Mysteries of the Kingdom

Mysteries of the Kingdom

by

Bruce E. Dana

ISBN: 1-55517-527-9
v.2

Published by Bonneville Books

Distributed by:
925 North Main, Springville, UT 84663 • 801/489-4084

CFI Publishing and Distribution Since 1986

Cedar Fort, Incorporated
CFI Distribution • CFI Books • Council Press • Bonneville Books

Typeset by Virginia Reeder
Cover design by Adam Ford
Cover design © 2001 by Lyle Mortimer

Printed in the United States of America

Acknowledgments

To my wife, Brenda, and my sons, Benjamin and Nathan, I express my love and appreciation; especially for allowing me time to research and write this work. Likewise, I express my love to my six daughters, Janalene, Connie, Michelle, Tami, Heather, and Brooke, for their love and devotion. I am eternally grateful for my parents, Edward K. and P. Shirley Dana, and my sister, Evelyn Giles, for their constant love and encouragement. Their devotion to the Church has instilled in me a love for the Church and its true teachings.

I am especially grateful for my dear friend, Dennis "C" Davis, who, for thirty years, has generously shared his vast knowledge of the gospel with me. Regarding my manuscript, I greatly appreciated his constructive criticism and helpful insights. Other trusted friends, James Peterson, Stephen Balls, Vaughn Cook, and Jean Britt, have read portions of my manuscript and given valuable comments and recommendations.

In particular, I am indebted to the leaders of the Church who have explained the gospel so plainly yet powerfully. This book is the result of their inspired teachings and doctrines. I want all to know that I revere and sustain the leaders of The Church of Jesus Christ of Latter-day Saints.

*****

CONTENTS

* * * * * *

Preface

Alma, who is the son of Alma, reveals this verity in the Book of Mormon:

> "It is given unto many to know the *mysteries of God;*
>
> . . . he that will harden his heart, the same receiveth the lesser portion of the word; and he that will not harden his heart, to him is given the greater portion of the word, until it is given unto him to *know the mysteries of God until he know them in full.*" (Alma 12: 9-10. Italics added)

According to a dictionary definition, a mystery is something that is unexplained. Matters of science, philosophy, or doctrine may be a mystery to one individual but not to another. Even the first principles and ordinances of the gospel—faith, repentance, baptism by immersion, and the laying on of hands for the gift of the Holy Ghost—may be a mystery to various people. Once a person understands a principle or doctrine, it is no longer a mystery.

Regarding mysteries of the kingdom, the Lord revealed:

> "If thou shalt ask, thou shalt receive revelation upon revelation, *knowledge upon knowledge,* that thou mayest *know the mysteries* and peaceable

things—that which bringeth joy, that which bringeth life eternal.

. . . for unto you it is given to *know the mysteries of the kingdom,* but unto the world it is not given to know them. (D&C 42: 61, 65; see also D&C 76: 5-10. Italics added)

Whenever I quote leaders of the Church in this work, it is the right and responsibility of the reader to compare those quoted expressions with the scriptures found in the four Standard Works of the Church, the words of the prophets, and official declarations issued by the First Presidency of the Church. Then, through personal study and prayer, the reader can determine if the Brethrens' statements are their own opinion or inspired words of truth.

The purpose of this work is not to sensationalize sacred gospel teachings. It is written to help the reader gain a greater understanding and appreciation for Mormon doctrine seldom mentioned.

After relating some marvelous experiences, President Brigham Young justified his telling by explaining:

"Now, you may think I am unwise in publicly telling these things, thinking perhaps I should preserve them in my own breast; but such is not my mind. *I would like the people called Latter-day Saints to understand some little things with regard to the workings and dealings of the Lord with his people here upon the earth.*" (A discourse of President Brigham Young, delivered at a special conference held at Farmington, Utah, on Sunday, June 17, 1877, as recorded in *Journal of Discourses,* Volume 19, pp. 36-39. Italics added) For the same reason expressed by President Young, I have written *Mysteries of the Kingdom.* I assume sole and full responsibility for the interpretations in this work.

—Bruce E. Dana

ARTICLE ONE

How God The Father Became Our God

With the Spirit as our guide, let us discover how God the Father became our God. From the Prophet Joseph Smith, we learn these grand and marvelous truths:

> *"It is necessary for us to have an understanding of God himself in the beginning.* If we start right, it is easy to go right all the time; but if we start wrong, we may go wrong, and it will be a hard matter to get right . . .
>
> "If men do not comprehend the character of God they do not comprehend themselves . . .
>
> "My first object is to find out the character of the only wise and true God, *and what kind of being he is . . .*
>
> "I am going to inquire after God; [Please note these next words:] *for I want you all to know him and to be familiar with him . . .* I speak as one having authority . . ." (*Journal of Discourses*, Volume 6: 2-3; April 6, 1844. Italics added)

It needs to be emphasized that Joseph Smith saw

1

God the Father and his Son, in the Sacred Grove, and he speaks with authority as an eyewitness of them. The Prophet then gives this powerful yet logical explanation of how God the Father became our God:

> "*God himself was once as we are now*, and is an exalted Man, and sits enthroned in yonder heavens. *That is the great secret.* If the vail was rent today, and the great God who holds this world in its orbit, and who upholds all worlds and all things by his power, was to make himself visible, —*I say, if you were to see him today, you would see him like a man in form*—like yourselves, in all the person, image, and very form as a man; for Adam was created in the very fashion, image, and likeness of God, and received instruction from, and walked, talked, and conversed with him, as one man talks and communes with another . . .

> "*I am going to tell you how God came to be God.* We have imagined and supposed that God was God from all eternity. I will refute that idea, and will take away and do away the vail, so that you may see.

> "These are incomprehensible ideas to some; but they are simple. It is the first principle of the Gospel to know for a certainty the character of God and to know that we may converse with him as one man converses with another, *and that he was once a man like us; yea, that God himself, the Father of us all, dwelt on an earth the same as Jesus Christ himself did* . . . What did Jesus say? . . . The Scriptures inform us that Jesus said, 'As the Father hath power

in himself, even so hath the Son power'—to do what? Why, what the Father did. The answer is obvious—in a manner, *to lay down his body and take it up again.*" [See John 10: 17-18]

Please note these revealing words:

"*Jesus, what are you going to do? To lay down my life, as my Father did, and take it up again.* Do you believe it? If you do not believe it, you do not believe the Bible. The Scriptures say it, and I defy all the learning and wisdom and all the combined powers of earth and hell together to refute it.

"Here, then, is eternal life—to know the only wise and true God; and *you have got to learn how to be Gods yourselves*, and to be kings and priests to God, *the same as all Gods have done before you,—* namely, by going from one small degree to another, and from a small capacity to a great one,—from grace to grace, from exaltation to exaltation, *until you attain to the resurrection of the dead*, and are able to dwell in everlasting burnings and to sit in glory, *as do those who sit enthroned in everlasting power.*" (*Journal of Discourses,* Volume 6: 3-4; April 6, 1844. Italics added)

Again it must be emphasized that the passage "*to lay down his body and take it up again*" does not, as some have supposed, mean that the Father was the Savior on his particular world. It could simply mean that he laid down his body in death and took it up again in the resurrection.

This is even supported in the paragraph where it states that individuals become "Gods" by attaining "the resurrection of the dead."

Elder Orson Pratt

In conjunction with what the Prophet Joseph Smith has revealed, Elder Orson Pratt uses inspired questions and logic to support the same conclusion:

> "A great many have supposed that God the Eternal Father, whom we worship in connection with his Son, Jesus Christ, was always a self-existing, eternal being from all eternity, that he had no beginning as a personage. But in order to illustrate this [point], let us inquire, *What is our destiny*? Our bodies will be glorified in the same manner as his body is . . .
>
> "Says one, to carry it out still further, 'if we become gods and are glorified like unto him, our bodies fashioned like unto his most glorious body, *may not he* [God the Father] *have passed through a mortal ordeal as we mortals are now doing? Why not?*" (*Journal of Discourses*, Volume 18, pp. 292-293; November 12, 1876)

An Inspired Couplet

The following address by Elder Lorenzo Snow not only endorses what the Prophet Joseph Smith has revealed, but condenses the truth of his message into a couplet.

"I had been in this Church but a short time when I succeeded in securing the *most perfect knowledge* that there was a God, that there was a Son, Jesus Christ, and that Joseph Smith was acknowledged of God and His prophet. It was a *knowledge* that no man could communicate. It came through a revelation from the Almighty . . .

"It is a long time since the knowledge of which I speak was communicated to me in a vision. But it has not been forgotten. When it was first shown to me it was *personal property*; I dared not communicate it. It was something that I had never heard before. Now, however, it is *public property*. It seems, after all the education that we have had in things pertaining to the celestial worlds, that there are some Latter-day Saints who are so well satisfied with simply knowing that the work is true that when you come to talk to them of our great future they seem surprised, and think it is nothing to do partic- ularly with them.

"Now I will say what I received in vision, which was just as clear as the sun ever shone. The knowledge that was communicated to me I embraced in this couplet:

**'As man now is, God once was.
As God now is, man may be.'**

"That is a very wonderful thing. It was to me. I did not know but that I had come into possession of knowledge that I had no business with; *but I knew it was true.* Nothing of this kind had ever reached my ears before. It was preached a few years after that; at least, the Prophet Joseph Smith taught this idea to the Twelve Apostles. Now, however, it is *common property;* but I do not know how many there are here that have got *a real knowledge of these things in their hearts.*" (October 5, 1894, *Millennial Star* 56: 770, 772; December 3, 1894. Italics and bold letters added)

Accordingly, God was born as a mortal man on an earth. By his faithfulness and valiancy to the laws and commandments of his Heavenly Father and God, he was—after his mortal death and subsequent resurrection—crowned a God. Then, he became our Heavenly Father and God.

* * * * * *

ARTICLE TWO

Is Our Savior The Redeemer Of Many Worlds?

Without a lengthy discussion on the atonement, we will consider whether our Savior is the *redeemer* of many worlds, or this earth only. It has been taught that when our Lord atoned for our sins, both in Gethsemane and on the cross, that this transcendent of all events applies to an infinite number of worlds. For a better understanding of this teaching, the reader is referred to two works written by Elder Bruce R. McConkie, *Mormon Doctrine*, 2nd ed., p. 65, and *A New Witness for the Articles of Faith*, pp. 130-131.

Let us consider another point of view, as we read these thought-provoking words of President Brigham Young about "a divine debt" and "a divine sacrifice:"

> "Our first parents transgressed the law that was given them in the garden; their eyes were opened. This created the *debt*. What is the nature of this *debt*? It is a *divine debt*. What will pay it? I ask, Is there anything short of a *divine sacrifice* that can pay this debt? No; there is not.

". . . A divine debt has been contracted by the children, [Adam and Eve, as well as all His spirit children] and the Father demands recompense. *He says to his children on this earth, who are in sin and transgression, it is impossible for you to pay this debt; I have prepared a sacrifice; I will send my Only Begotten Son to pay this divine debt* . . . the Divine Father, whom we serve, the God of the Universe, the God and Father of our Lord Jesus Christ, and the Father of our spirits, provided this sacrifice and sent his Son to die for us; and it is also a great fact that the Son came to do the will of the Father, *and that he has paid the debt,* in fulfillment of the Scripture which says, 'He was the Lamb slain from the foundation of the world.'"[Rev. 13: 8]

Then, using logic and wisdom, President Young expounds this great mystery:

"*Is it so on any other earth? . . . Sin is upon every earth that ever was created,* and if it was not so, I would like some philosophers to let us know how people can be exalted to become sons of God, and enjoy a fullness of glory with the Redeemer. *Consequently **every earth has its redeemer**, and every earth has its tempter*; and every earth, and the people thereof, in their turn and time, receive all that we receive, and pass through all the ordeals that we are passing through.

"Is this easy to understand? It is perfectly easy to me; and my advice to those who have queries and doubts on this subject is, when they reason and philosophize upon it, not to plant their position in falsehood or argue hypothetically, but upon the facts as they exist . . ." (*Journal of Discourses*, Volume 14, pp. 71-72; July 10, 1870. Italics and bold lettering added)

Because "sin is upon every earth that ever was created," the reader will have to determine if President Young was eloquently teaching that every earth has its redeemer, and that our Savior's atonement covers infinite number of earths, or, that every earth has its *own individual* redeemer.

* * * * * *

ARTICLE THREE

Gods Are Eternal

When did Gods come into existence? Let us read what has been revealed on this intriguing subject. From the Prophet Joseph Smith, we obtain this doctrine:

"Our text says, 'And hath made us kings and priests unto *God and His Father*' [Rev.1:6]. The Apostles have discovered that there were Gods above, for Paul says God was the Father of our Lord Jesus Christ. My object was to preach the scriptures, and preach the doctrine they contain, *there being a God above, the Father of our Lord Jesus Christ.* I am bold to declare I have taught all the strong doctrines publicly, and always teach stronger doctrines in public than in private." (Joseph Fielding Smith, comp.,*Teachings of the Prophet Joseph Smith,* 1938, p. 370. Italics added)

He further explains, ". . . If Jesus Christ was the Son of God, and *John discovered that God the Father of Jesus Christ had a Father, you may suppose that He had a Father also.* Where was there ever a son without a father? . . . *Hence if Jesus had a*

Father, can we not believe that He had a Father also?" (Ibid., p. 373. Italics added)

Regarding Gods and endless time, Elder Orson Pratt provides this revealing information:

> "If it is necessary for us to obtain experience through the things that are presented before us in this life, why not those beings, who are already exalted and become gods, obtain their experience in the same way? We would find, were we to carry this subject from world to world, from our world to another, even to the *endless ages of eternity, that there never was a time but what there was a Father and Son.* In other words, when you entertain that which is *endless,* you exclude the idea of a first being, a first world; the moment you admit of a first, you limit the idea of endless. The chain itself is endless, but each link had its beginning."

He then presents doctrines that are difficult for mortals to understand. To explain, from the time that we are born, we are taught, and we experience, that all things upon this earth have a beginning and an end. Further, everything is based on time. With this understanding, we continue again with Elder Pratt's inspired explanation:

> "Says one, 'This is incomprehensible.' It may be in some respects. We can admit, though, that *duration is endless,* for it is impossible for man to conceive of a limit to it. *If duration is endless, there*

can never be a first minute, a first hour, or first period; endless duration in the past is made up of a continuation of endless successive moments—it had no beginning. Precisely so with regard to this endless succession of personages; *there never will be a time when fathers, and sons, and worlds will not exist* ; neither was there ever a period through all the past ages of duration, *but . . . there [existed] a world, and a Father and Son, a redemption and exaltation to the fullness and power of the Godhead."* (*Journal of Discourses*, Volume 18, p. 293; November 12, 1876)

From these inspired teachings, it is apparent that there never was a time when there was not a "Godhead." Further, it is also apparent that Gods are eternal.

* * * * * *

ARTICLE FOUR

Adam:
"A Son Of God"

One of the most intriguing yet misunderstood doctrines of the Church is how Adam came into this world. With the Spirit as our guide, we will find out what is contained in Holy Writ, and by inspired men of God.

In the book of Genesis, we read these informative words:

"And God said, Let us make man in our image, after our likeness:

"So God created man in his own image, in the image of God created he him; male and female created he them." (Gen. 1: 26-27)

These scriptures have a dual meaning. The first pertains to Adam and Eve specifically; the second pertains to mankind in general. Both Adam and Eve were created in the image of our Eternal Father and Mother in Heaven. Likewise, all of mankind is created in the image of our Eternal Parents.

In the second chapter of Genesis, we read these interesting words about Adam:

> "And the Lord God formed man of the dust of the ground, and breathed into his nostrils the breath of life; and man became a living soul.
>
> "And the Lord God planted a garden eastward in Eden; and there he put the man whom he had formed." (Gen. 2: 7-8. See also Moses 2 and 3)

From these scriptures, a person could infer that Adam was formed of the dust of the ground, in the image of God. Regarding the word "formed," let us read these clarifying words:

> ". . . mankind has been prone ever since the fall, as it is called, to take hold of the things of the earth and neglect to a large extent the things of the heavens . . . *but we find that we are . . . the children of the great Eternal Father in the spirit, and born here on the earth in the regular order according to the laws of generation, from the time of our father Adam downward,* for a purpose; and what is that? *That we might obtain a body formed out of these lower elements* and through that body be able to obtain experiences that we could not obtain in our first or spiritual estate." (Charles W. Penrose, of the First Presidency. An address, August 8, 1915, *Deseret News Semi-Weekly,* no. 54, p. 9, August 26, 1915. Italics and boldface added)

From this explanation, we understand that all people, from "Adam downward" are "born here on the earth in
the regular order according to the laws of generation" [in
other words: by the process of procreation] and that we
"obtain a body *formed* out of these lower elements." How
are we formed? To answer, we are "born" and "formed" in
the image of God, and our "formed" bodies contain elements similar to those elements found in the earth.

The pedigree of Christ was traced by the Apostle
Luke to "Enos, which was *the* son of Seth, which was *the*
son of *Adam, which was the son of God.*" (Luke 3: 38.
Italics added) To support this pedigree, we read in the book
of Moses: "And this is the genealogy of the sons of *Adam,
who was the son of God*, with whom God, himself, conversed." (Moses 6: 22. Italics added)

If Adam is a "son of God," how can Christ be the
"Only Begotten Son" of the Father in the flesh? (See Moses
1:6,17,31,33; Jac. 4:5,11; Alma 12:33-34, 13:5; D&C 20:21;
29:42) Was not Adam born before Christ?

President Brigham Young has revealed this marvelous information about those who are valiant in this life
and are crowned to be a God:

"We have not the power in the flesh to create
and bring forth or produce a spirit; but we have the
power to produce a temporal body. The germ of this,
God has placed within us. And when our spirits
receive our bodies, and through our faithfulness we

are worthy to be crowned, we will then receive authority to *produce both spirit and body.*" (*Journal of Discourses*, Volume 15, p. 137; Aug. 24, 1872. Italics added)

In a course of study of the Church, *Divine Mission of the Savior*, we read these interesting comments:

"THE CREATION OF ADAM AND EVE— One of the important points about the topic is to learn, if possible, how *Adam obtained his body of flesh and bones. There would seem to be but one natural and reasonable explanation, and that is, that Adam obtained his body in the same way Christ obtained his—and just as all men obtain theirs—namely, by being born of woman.*" (Course of study for Priests—1910. Italics added. Prepared and issued under the direction of The General Authorities of the Church—December 4, 1909. The General Committee consists of Rudger Clawson, David O. McKay, Seymour B. Young, B. H. Roberts, Rulon S. Wells, Joseph W. McMurrin, Charles W. Nibley, etc., p. 37)

In harmony with this statement, the First Presidency of the Church has written:

"Adam, our great progenitor, 'the first man,' was, like Christ, a pre-existent spirit, and like Christ he took upon him an appropriate body, the body of a man, and so became a 'living soul.' . . . and that all who have inhabited the earth since Adam have taken bodies and become souls in like manner . . . Man began life as a human being, in the likeness of our heavenly father.

"True it is that the body of man enters upon its career as a tiny germ or embryo, which becomes an infant, quickened at a certain stage by the spirit whose tabernacle it is, and the child, after being born, develops into a man. There is nothing in this, however, to indicate that *the original man, the first of our race, began life as anything less than a man, or less than the human germ or embryo that becomes a man.*" (Joseph F. Smith, John R. Winder, Anthon H. Lund, *The Improvement Era* 13:80; November 1909)

Then, without reservation, President Joseph F. Smith declares:

"The Son, Jesus Christ, grew and developed into manhood the same as you or I, as likewise did God, His Father, grow and develop to the Supreme Being that He now is. Man was born of woman; Christ, the Savior, was born of woman; and God, the Father, was born of woman. *Adam, our earthly parent, was also born of woman into this world, the same as Jesus and you and I.*" (An address, December 7, 1913, *Deseret Evening News*, December 27, 1913, p. 7, also quoted in *Church News Section*, Sept. 19, 1936, pp. 2, 8)

In a letter, the First Presidency writes:

"Salt Lake City, UTAH

February 20, 1912

Pres. Samuel O. Bennion

Independence, Missouri

Dear Brother:

Your question concerning Adam has not been answered because of pressure of important business . . .

"If you will carefully examine the sermon to which you refer . . . you will discover that. . . President Young denied that Jesus was 'begotten by the Holy Ghost' . . .

"President Young went on to show that our *father Adam*—that is, our earthly father—the progenitor of the race of man, stands at the head, being 'Michael the Archangel, the Ancient of Days,' *and that he was not fashioned from earth like an adobe, but begotten by his Father in Heaven.*

Your brethren, Joseph F. Smith

Anthon H. Lund

Charles W. Penrose, First Presidency."

(*Man: His Origin And Destiny, by Joseph Fielding Smith*, p. 344. Also found in: *Messages of The First Presidency*, Volume 4, p. 266)

Now, how do we resolve that Adam is a "son of God" yet Jesus Christ is the "Only Begotten Son of the Father in the flesh?" To answer this intriguing question, we rely upon the apostolic wisdom of Elder Bruce R. McConkie:

"Christ is the *Son of God*; and he has been so designated from the beginning to show the personal, intimate, family relationship that exists between him and his Father . . .

"*Father Adam*, the first man, is also a *son of God* (Luke 3:38; Moses 6:22, 59), a fact that does not change the great truth that Christ is the Only Begotten in the flesh, *for Adam's entrance into this world was in immortality.* He came here before death had its beginning, with its consequent mortal or flesh-status of existence." (*Mormon Doctrine*, 2nd ed., 1966, 1986 p. 742. Italics added)

Because the Father and his Eternal Companion can *produce both spirit and body* children, Adam is a "son of God," the same as Jesus Christ is a "Son of God." The difference is that *Adam* [and we must add Eve also] *was born in immortality*, upon this earth, from God the Father and our Mother in Heaven. Jesus Christ was born in mortality, upon this earth, from God the Father and the mortal woman, Mary.

* * * * * *

ARTICLE FIVE

Jesus Christ
was
Naturally Begotten

There are many people who do not properly understand or accept as the truth that the conception of Jesus Christ was accomplished by a literal union between God the Father and the mortal Mary. With the Spirit as our guide, we will present doctrines that relate to this holy subject.

What does it mean to be naturally begotten? To answer, we use expressions from three General Authorities. Elder Heber C. Kimball provides the following information:

"I will say that I was naturally begotten; so was my father, and also my Saviour Jesus Christ. According to the Scriptures, he is the first begotten of his father in the flesh, and there was nothing unnatural about it." (*Journal of Discourses*, Volume 8, p. 211; September 2, 1860)

From President Brigham Young, we read:

"The birth of the Saviour was as natural as are the births of our children; it was the result of natural action. He partook of flesh and blood—was begotten of his Father, as we were of our fathers." (*Journal of Discourses*, Volume 8, p. 115; July 8, 1860)

From Elder Bruce R. McConkie, we come to understand:

". . . Christ was begotten by an Immortal Father in the same way that mortal men are begotten by mortal Fathers." (*Mormon Doctrine*, 2nd ed., Bookcraft, 1966. Copyright 1966, 1986 by Bookcraft, Inc., p. 547. Used by permission)

Elder Bruce R. McConkie further writes:

". . . There is nothing figurative about his paternity; he was begotten, conceived and born in the normal and natural course of events, for he is the Son of God, and that designation means what it says. (Ibid., p. 742)

From these plainly spoken words, it should be clear that Jesus was begotten by his Heavenly Father in the same way that all men and women in mortality are begotten of their earthly parents. In addition, it should be clear also that the conception of Jesus Christ was the result of a literal union between God the Father and the precious and chosen vessel, Mary.

* * * * * *

ARTICLE SIX

Jesus Christ is
born of a Virgin

The scriptures emphasize that Mary was a virgin. This includes the time before and after the birth of Jesus, until she was known by her husband, Joseph (See Matt. 1: 24-25). The question naturally arises, *if indeed the Father and Mary conceived Jesus by a literal union, how could Mary remain a virgin?* To answer this intriguing question, we turn once again to Elder Bruce R. McConkie for explanation:

"Mary was a virgin . . . until after the birth of our Lord. Then, for the first time, she was known by Joseph, her husband; and other children, both sons and daughters, were then born to her. (Matt. 13:55-56; Mark 6:3; Gal. 1:19) *She conceived and brought forth her Firstborn Son while yet a virgin because the Father of that child was an immortal personage.*" (*Doctrinal New Testament Commentary, Volume 1: The Gospels,* Bookcraft, 1965. Copyright 1965 by Bookcraft, Inc. p. 82. Used by permission. Italics added)

From this explanation, we learn that Mary's virginity was retained by the fact that the conception of Jesus Christ was a union between a mortal woman and an Immortal Man. Mary ceased being a virgin when she was "known by Joseph, her husband" because that particular union was between a mortal man and a mortal woman. (See Matt. 1:25)

* * * * * *

ARTICLE SEVEN

Jesus Christ's Conception
is Not Degrading

Some individuals may believe that if there were a literal union between the Father and Mary that this act would degrade God and debauch Mary. Elder Melvin J. Ballard gives this inspired explanation:

"Mary told the story most beautifully when she said that an angel of the Lord came to her and told her that she had found favor in the sight of God, and had come to be worthy of the fulfillment of the promises heretofore made, to become the virgin mother of the Redeemer of the world. She afterwards, referring to the event, said: 'God hath done wonderful things unto me.' 'And the Holy Ghost came upon her,' is the story, 'and she came into the presence of the highest.' No man or woman can live in mortality and survive the presence of the Highest except by the sustaining power of the Holy Ghost. So it came upon her to prepare her for admittance into the divine presence, and the power of the Highest, who is the Father, was present, and overshadowed her, and the holy Child that was born of her was called the Son of God.

"Men who deny this, or who think it degrades our Father, have no true conception of the sacredness of the most marvelous power with which God has endowed mortal men—the power of creation. Even though that power may be abused and may become a mere harp of pleasure to the wicked, nevertheless it is the most sacred and holy and divine function with which God has endowed man. Made holy, it is retained by the Father of us all, and in his exercise of that great and marvelous creative power and function, he did not debase himself, degrade himself, nor debauch his daughter. Thus Christ became the literal Son of a divine Father, and no one else was worthy to be his father." (Bryant S. Hinckley, *Sermons and Missionary Services of Melvin Joseph Ballard* (Salt Lake City: Deseret Book, 1949), pp. 166-167. Used by permission)

From these inspired and enlightening words, we understand that mortals view the creative power differently than the Father, for as Isaiah has well written: "For my thoughts *are* not your thoughts, neither *are* your ways my ways, saith the Lord" (Isa. 55:8). Elder Ballard has explained it so plainly, yet powerfully, that the creative power is the most sacred, holy, and divine function that can be performed by man and God.

God the Father is the most holy, righteous, and pure-minded Man of all men. Further, he has the most respect for women and womanhood above all others. When Mary was in his presence and he overshadowed her, he performed a most sacred and holy function, with divine tenderness, love, and respect. Thereby, he did not degrade or debase himself or Mary.

This most righteous woman knew why she was in the Father's presence. Gabriel explained this to her while she was in Nazareth. Would we be wrong to believe that she and the Spirit communicated about sacred things while she was being bodily transported to the presence of the Highest? Further, would it be unreasonable to believe that for a short length of time the veil was taken from her mind and she was able to see the presentation of the Father's plan of salvation before his spirit children, as well as her own calling to be the mortal mother of Jesus Christ? Although not supported by any revealed knowledge, is there any doubt that very rapidly in the Highest's presence his thoughts became her thoughts and his ways became her ways (Isa. 55:8). Further, even though Mary knew she was espoused to Joseph, she felt no shame, coercion, uneasiness, or hesitancy to become the mother of our Lord. This precious and chosen vessel, willing and without reservation, became the mother of Jesus Christ because of her total love and obedience to the Father and his plan of salvation, which plan calls for a Savior and Redeemer. Accordingly, in this most sacred setting, and by their holy union, Mary conceived in her womb God's Son.

* * * * * *

ARTICLE EIGHT

Relationship of
Mary and the Father

Regarding gospel mysteries, we shall learn of one that is the least spoken of or understood. Three General Authorities have expressed marvelous and thought-provoking comments regarding the relationship between God the Father and Mary. With the Spirit as our guide, let us discover what has been revealed on this holy and sacred subject.

Elder Orson Pratt

From Elder Orson Pratt, we read these thought-provoking words:

"The fleshly body of Jesus required a Mother as well as a Father. Therefore, the Father and Mother of Jesus, according to the flesh, must have been associated together in the capacity of Husband and Wife; hence the Virgin Mary must have been, for the time being, the *lawful* wife of God the Father: we use the term *lawful* Wife, because it would be blasphemous in the highest degree to say that He over-

27

shadowed her or begat the Saviour unlawfully. It would have been unlawful for any *man* to have interfered with Mary, who was already espoused to Joseph; for such a heinous crime would have subjected both the guilty parties to death, according to the law of Moses. But God having created all men and women, had the most perfect right to do with His own creation, according to His holy will and pleasure: He had a lawful right to overshadow the Virgin Mary in the capacity of a husband, and beget a Son, although she was espoused to another; for the law which He gave to govern men and women was not intended to govern Himself, or to prescribe rules for his own conduct. It was also lawful in Him, after having thus dealt with Mary, to give her to Joseph her espoused husband. Whether God the Father gave Mary to Joseph for time only, or for time and eternity, we are not informed. Inasmuch as God was the first husband to her, it may be that He only gave her to be the wife of Joseph while in this mortal state, and that He intended after the resurrection to again take her as one of his own wives to raise up immortal spirits in eternity." (*The Seer*, Washington D.C. Edition; October 1853, p. 158)

In the next monthly publication, Elder Pratt further writes:

"We have now clearly shown that God the Father had a plurality of wives, one or more being in eternity, by whom He begat our spirits as well as the spirit of Jesus His First Born, and another being upon the earth by whom He begat the tabernacle of Jesus, as His Only Begotten in this world." (Ibid., p. 172; November, 1853)

(Elder Orson Pratt was ordained an Apostle, April 26, 1835. He died October 3, 1881.)

President Brigham Young

In addition to Elder Pratt's comments, President Brigham Young has spoken these revealing words:

"The man Joseph, the husband of Mary, did not, that we know of, have more than one wife, but Mary the wife of Joseph had another husband . . . That very babe that was cradled in the manger, was begotten, not by Joseph, the husband of Mary, but by another Being. Do you inquire by whom? He was begotten by God our heavenly Father." (*Journal of Discourses*, Volume 11, p. 268; August 19, 1866)

(Brigham Young became President of the Church, December 27, 1847 and was the Lord's prophet until his death, August 29, 1877.)

President Joseph F. Smith

Lastly, President Joseph F. Smith has declared:

"Mary was married to Joseph for *time*. No man could take her for *eternity* because she belonged to the Father of her divine Son." (An address given at Box Elder Stake Conference, December 20, 1914; printed in *Box Elder News* of January 28, 1915)

(Joseph F. Smith became President of the Church, October 17, 1901 and was the Lord's prophet until his death, November 19, 1918.)

From these enlightening expressions, the reader will have to determine whether "the Father and Mother of Jesus, according to the flesh, . . . [are] associated together in the capacity of Husband and Wife." Whatever their relationship may be, this holy and sacred event transpired exactly as Gabriel had told Mary in Nazareth:

"The Holy Ghost shall come upon thee, and the power of the Highest shall overshadow thee: therefore also that holy thing [child] which shall be born of thee shall be called the Son of God." (Luke 1:35)

* * * * * *

ARTICLE NINE

Jesus, at Age Twelve
(See Luke 2: 43-50)

Do we fully understand and appreciate the greatness of our Lord? Due to his valiancy in the premortal life, he was foreordained to be the Savior and Redeemer of all mankind. He was the Great Jehovah of the Old Testament. On earth, he was given the sacred and holy name of Jesus Christ. Though he was born as a mortal, he still retained his Godship. He came into this world with talents, abilities, and spiritual endowments far exceeding any mortal. Being sinless, our Lord was constantly in tune with his Father in Heaven. Because he was the "Only Begotten Son" of the Father in the flesh, who was more qualified to teach him than his Father? His knowledge and understanding came quickly and abundantly. At age twelve, he could reason with the wisest doctors of divinity. From the Prophet Joseph Smith, we learn these great truths:

". . . but it is not always wise to relate all the truth. Even Jesus, the Son of God, had to refrain from doing so, and had to restrain His feelings many times for the safety of Himself and His followers, and had to conceal the righteous purposes of His heart in relation to many things pertaining to His Father's kingdom. *When still a boy He had all the intelligence necessary to enable Him to rule and govern the kingdom of the Jews, and could reason with the wisest and most profound doctors of law and divinity, and make their theories and practice appear like folly compared with the wisdom He possessed;* but He was a boy only, and lacked physical strength even to defend His own person; and was subject to cold, to hunger and to death." (Joseph Fielding Smith, comp., *Teachings of the Prophet Joseph Smith*, 1938, p. 392. Italics added)

* * * * * *

ARTICLE TEN

Is Our Savior Married?

The question of whether our Savior is married is a sensitive and seldom-discussed mystery of the gospel. Therefore, let us learn what has been revealed on this holy and sacred subject.

From the article in this work entitled "Adam: A son of God," we know that God the Father is not a single parent. We further know that he is married and lives in a family unit.

The Church of Jesus Christ of Latter-day Saints teaches that the basic unit of the Church is the family. The First Presidency and Council of the Twelve Apostles issued a marvelous document, titled, *A Proclamation To The World*. In it, we read important doctrines about God's law, especially about marriage, chastity, and taking care of children. It emphasizes strongly that the family unit is approved by God, and that marriage is a necessary part of Heavenly Father's plan. (delivered Sept. 23, 1995, President Gordon B. Hinckley)

From the Doctrine and Covenants, we read about

the new and everlasting covenant of marriage:

"For behold, I reveal unto you a new and an everlasting covenant; and if ye abide not that covenant, then are ye damned; for no one can reject this covenant and be permitted to enter into my glory.

"For all who will have a blessing at my hands shall abide the law which was appointed for that blessing, *and the conditions thereof, as were instituted from before the foundation of the world . . .*

"Behold, mine house is a house of order, saith the Lord God, and not a house of confusion...

"And again, verily I say unto you, if a man marry a wife by my word, which is my law, and by the new and everlasting covenant, and it is sealed unto them by the Holy Spirit of promise, . . . Ye shall come forth in the first resurrection; . . . and they shall pass by the angels, and the gods, which are set there, *to their exaltation and glory in all things, as hath been sealed upon their heads, which glory shall be a fullness and a continuation of the seeds forever and ever.*

"Then shall they be gods, because they have no end; therefore shall they be from everlasting to everlasting, because they continue; then shall they be above all, because all things are subject unto them. Then shall they be gods, because they have all power, and the angels are subject unto them." (D&C 132: 4-5; 8; 19-20. Italics added)

From the proclamation issued by the Church, which

was inspired by our Lord; and the new and everlasting covenant of marriage which was revealed to the Prophet Joseph Smith, from our Lord, it is reasonable to believe that our Savior is married, for he himself declared, *"for no one can reject this covenant and be permitted to enter into my glory."*

With this introduction, let us discover what has been revealed by the leaders of the Church.

> ". . . Christ could not have fulfilled His mission here if He had not been set apart and ordained here as well as in the heavens, and baptized and prepared through obedience to the law of God *to set an example in all things to the people.* Christ, therefore, went unto John to be baptized. John forbade Him; but Jesus said, 'Suffer it to be so now: for thus it becometh us to fulfill all righteousness' [See Matt. 3:15]. Jesus Christ *never omitted the fulfillment of a single law that God has made known for the salvation of the children of men.* It would not have done for Him to have come and obeyed one law and neglected or rejected another. He could not consistently do that and then say to mankind, 'Follow me.'" (President Joseph F. Smith, who then was a counselor in the First Presidency, An address, March 20, 1899, *Millennial Star* 62: 97, February 15, 1900)

Then, a valid question is asked by Elder Orson Hyde: *"When does it say the Savior was married?* I believe I will read it for your accommodation, or you might not believe my words were I to say that there is indeed such a scripture[:]

> "We will turn over to the account of the marriage in Cana of Galilee, [See John 2: 1-12] and the mother of Jesus was there . . . Gentlemen, that is as plain as the translators, or different councils over this Scripture, dare allow it to go to the world, but [the] thing is there; it is told; Jesus was the bridegroom at the marriage of Cana of Galilee, and he told them what to do.
>
> "Now there was actually a marriage; and if Jesus was not the bridegroom on that occasion, please tell who was. If any man can show this, and prove that it was not the Savior of the world, then I will acknowledge I am in error. *We say it was Jesus Christ who was married . . .*" (The Marriage Relations, *Journal of Discourses*, Volume 2:82; October 6, 1854. Italics added)

In this same lecture, Elder Hyde promotes the doctrine that not only was Christ married, but that he was a polygamist and had children:

> "Our first parents, then, were commanded to multiply and replenish the earth; and if the Savior found it his duty to be baptized to fulfill all righteousness, a command of far less importance than that of multiplying his race . . . would he not find it his duty to join in with the rest of the faithful ones in replenishing the earth? [He then asks this of himself] 'Mr. Hyde, *do you really wish to imply that the immaculate Savior begat children?*' . . . This is the

general idea; but the Savior never thought it beneath him to obey the mandate of his Father; . . . [Again, he asks himself] *'Then you really mean to hold to the doctrine that the Savior of the world was married*; do you mean to be understood so? And if so, do you mean to be understood that *he had more than one wife?'* . . .

"There is an old prophecy of Isaiah . . . the 53rd chapter of his prophecies . . . This particular prophecy speaks of Christ all the way through. It is there said, 'When thou shalt make his soul an offering for sin, *he shall see his seed.'* [v.10. Italics added] . . . *If he has no seed, how could he see them?* . . . I shall say here, that before the Savior died, he looked upon his own natural children, as we look upon ours . . . they passed into the shades of obscurity, never to be exposed to mortal eye as the seed of the blessed one."

He then gives this insight:

"How was it with Mary and Martha, and other women that followed him? . . . When Mary of old came to the sepulchre . . . she saw two angels in white, 'And they say unto her, Woman, why weepest thou? She said unto them, Because they have taken away my Lord,' *or husband,* 'and I know not where they have laid him . . . ' [John 20: 11-18; Mark 16: 9-11] *Is there not here manifested the affections of a wife*[?] These words speak the kindred ties and sympathies that are common to that relation of husband

and wife. (*Journal of Discourses*, Volume 2: 79-82; October 6, 1854. Italics added)

Note: President Brigham Young was present at this meeting. At the end of Elder Hyde's remarks, President Young spoke these endorsing words:

"We have had a *splendid address* from brother Hyde, for which I am grateful. I feel in my heart to bless the people all the time, and can say *amen* to brother Hyde's last remarks . . .

"I say to the congregation, treasure up in your hearts what you have heard to-night [sic] . . . Elder Hyde says he has only just dipped into it, but, if it will not be displeasing to him, I will say he has not dipped into it yet; he has only run round the edge of the field. He has done so beautifully, and it will have its desired effect."(Ibid., p. 90; October 6, 1854. Italics added)

Speaking of his own lecture, Elder Hyde relates what was written by certain newspapers:

"I discover that some of the Eastern papers represent me as a great blasphemer, because I said, in my lecture on Marriage, at our last Conference, *that Jesus Christ was married at Cana of Galilee, that Mary, Martha,* and *others* were *his wives,* and that *he begat children.* All that I have to say in reply to that charge is this—they worship a Savior that is too pure and holy to fulfill the commands of his

Father. I worship one that is just pure and holy enough 'to fulfill all righteousness;' not only the righteous law of baptism, but the still *more righteous and important law 'to multiply and replenish the earth.'* Startle not at this! for even *the Father himself honored that law by coming down to Mary,* without a natural body, and begetting a son; and *if Jesus begat children, he only 'did that which he had seen his Father do.'"* (*Journal of Discourses*, Volume 2, p. 210; March 18, 1855)

Turning our attention to President Brigham Young, we read his sentiments on the subject of our Lord having wives and children:

"The Scripture says that He, the Lord, came walking in the Temple, with His train; I do not know who they were, unless *his wives and children*; . . ." [See Isaiah 6:1] (*Journal of Discourses*, Volume 13, p. 309; Nov. 13, 1870. Italics added)

In a publication, we read what Elder Orson Pratt wrote:

"Next let us inquire whether there are any intimations in Scripture concerning *the wives of Jesus* . . . One thing is certain, that there were several holy women that greatly loved Jesus—such as Mary, and Martha her sister, and Mary Magdalene; and Jesus greatly loved them, and associated with them much . . . If all the acts of Jesus were written, we, no doubt, should learn that these beloved woman *were his wives.*" (*The Seer*, October 1853. p. 159)

In this same publication, Elder Pratt writes these words:

". . . and when He arose from the dead, instead of first showing Himself to His chosen witnesses, the Apostles, He appeared first to these women, or at least to one of them—namely, Mary Magdalene. Now, it would be very natural for a *husband* in the resurrection to appear first to his own dear wives, and afterwards show himself to his other friends. If all the acts of Jesus were written, we no doubt should learn that these beloved women were his wives." (ibid.)

Lastly, we shall read what a member of the First Presidency has stated:

"Celsus was a heathen philosopher; and what does he say upon the subject of Christ and his Apostles, and their belief? He says, 'The grand reason why the Gentiles and philosophers of his school persecuted Jesus Christ, was, *because he had so many wives*; there were Elizabeth, and Mary, and a host of others that followed him.' After Jesus went from the stage of action, *the Apostles followed the example of their master* . . .

"The grand reason [for] the burst of public sentiment in anathemas upon Christ and his disciples, *causing his crucifixion, was evidently based upon polygamy,* according to the testimony of the philosophers who rose in that age. A belief in the doctrine of a plurality of wives caused the persecution of Jesus and his followers." (Jedediah M. Grant, Counselor in the First Presidency, *Journal of Discourses,* Volume 1: 345-346; August 7, 1853. Italics added)

Now, based on what has been spoken and written by early Church leaders, the reader will have to determine by prayer and by study if our Savior was married. Further, if he had wives and children.

* * * * * *

ARTICLE ELEVEN

Hidden Treasures,
and Stories of Porter Rockwell
and the
Hill Cumorah

Several years after the Saints arrived in the Salt Lake Valley, various men began to hunt for gold. Once this precious metal was discovered in California, many members of the Church left the valley to seek their fortune. President Brigham Young, and other Church leaders, counseled against this activity. In a Church meeting, President Young expressed his feelings on this subject and revealed "marvelous" experiences.

"When we consider the condition of the Latter-day Saints, and see how many there are who seem to have their eyes fixed upon the things of this world, things that are not lasting, but that perish in the handling, and how anxious they are to obtain them, how do you think I feel about it? We see many of the Elders of Israel desirous of becoming wealthy, and they adopt any course that they think will bring them riches, which to me is as unwise as anything can be—to see men of wisdom, men that seem to have an understanding of the world and of the things of God, searching after minerals throughout these mountains; they traverse the hills, and they dig here and there, and keep digging and picking, and rolling the rocks from morning till night. This chain of mountains has been followed from the north to the south, and its various spurs have been prospected, and what do they find? Just enough to allure them, and to finally lead them from the faith, and at last to make them miserable and poor. Ask the brethren why they do this, and the ready reply will be, 'Is it not my privilege to find a gold mine, or a silver mine, as well as others?' As far as I am concerned I would say, 'Yes, certainly it is your privilege, if you can find one.' But do you know how to find such a mine? No, you do not.'"

Later in his discourse, he declares:

"Now, should you go prospecting for gold or silver, you will find just enough to allure you and to destroy you . . . the man who is faithful to his calling and to this holy Priesthood, never goes hunting for gold or silver unless he is sent . . . People do not know it, but I know there is a seal set upon the treasures of the earth; men are allowed to go so far and no farther. I have known places where there were treasures in abundance; but could men get them? No. You can read in the Book of Mormon of the ancient Nephites holding their treasures, and of their becoming slippery; so that after they had privately hid their money, on going to the place again, lo and behold it was not there, but was somewhere else, but they knew not where."

Earlier in his discourse, he reveals a mystery that is not known:

"These treasures that are in the earth are carefully watched, they can be removed from place to place according to the good pleasure of Him who made and owns them. He has his messengers at his service, and it is just as easy for an angel to remove the minerals from any part of one of these mountains to another, as it is for you and me to walk up and down this hall. This, however, is not understood by the Christian world, nor by us as a people. There are certain circumstances that a number of my brethren and sisters have heard me relate, that will demonstrate this so positively, that none need doubt the truth of what I say."

Then, President Young begins to relate information about a particular gold mine in Utah:

"I presume there are some present who have heard me narrate a circumstance with regard to the discovery of a gold mine in Little Cottonwood [Canyon], and I will here say that the specimens taken from it, which I have in my possession today, are as fine specimens of gold as ever found on this continent. A man whom some of you will well know,

brought to me a most beautiful nugget. I told him to
let the mine alone.

Porter Rockwell

"When General [Patrick] Conner came here,
he did considerable prospecting; and in hunting
through the Cottonwoods, he had an inkling that
there was gold there. Porter [Orrin Porter Rockwell]
as we generally call him, came to me one day, saying,
'They have struck within four inches of my lode,
what shall I do?' He was carried away with the idea
that he must do something. I therefore told him to
go with the other brethren interested, and make his
claim. When he got through talking, I said to him,
'Porter, you ought to know better; you have seen and
heard things which I have not, and are a man of long
experience in this Church. I want to tell you one
thing; they may strike within four inches of that lode
as many times as they have a mind to, and they will
not find it.' They hunted and hunted, hundreds of
them did; and I had the pleasure of laughing at him
a little, for when he went there again, he could not
find it himself.' (Laughter)" [sic]

Then, another experience of Porter Rockwell:

"Sometimes I take the liberty of talking a little further with regard to such things. Orin [sic] P.
Rockwell is an eye-witness [sic] to some powers of
removing the treasures of the earth. He was with cer-

tain parties that lived nearby where the plates were found that contain the records of the Book of Mormon. There were a great many treasures hid up by the Nephites. Porter was with them one night where there were treasures, and they could find them easy enough, but they could not obtain them.

"I will tell you a story which will be marvelous to most of you. It was told me by Porter, whom I would believe just as quickly as any man that lives. When he tells a thing he understands, he will tell it just as he knows it; he is a man that does not lie. He said that on this night, when they were engaged hunting for this old treasure, they dug around the end of a chest for some twenty inches. The chest was about three feet square. One man who was determined to have the contents of that chest, took his pick and struck into the lid of it, and split through into the chest. The blow took off a piece of the lid, which a certain lady kept in her possession until she died. That chest of money went into the bank [embankment]. Porter describes it so [making a rumbling sound] [sic]; he says this is just as true as the heavens are. I have heard others tell the same story. I relate this because it is marvelous to you. But to those who understand these things, it is not marvelous.

"You hear a great deal said about finding money. There is no difficulty at all in finding money, but there are a great many people who do not know what to do with it when they do find it.

Hill Cumorah

"I lived right in the country where the plates were found from which the Book of Mormon was translated, and I know a great many things pertaining to that country. I believe I will take the liberty to tell you of another circumstance that will be as marvelous as anything can be. This is an incident in the life of Oliver Cowdery, but he did not take the liberty of telling such things in meeting as I take. I tell these things to you, and I have a motive for doing so. I want to carry them to the ears of my brethren and sisters, and to the children also, *that they may grow to an understanding of some things that seem to be entirely hidden from the human family.* Oliver Cowdery went with the Prophet Joseph when he deposited these plates. Joseph did not translate all of the plates; there was a portion of them sealed, which you can learn from the Book of Doctrine and Covenants. When Joseph got the plates, the angel instructed him to carry them back to the hill Cumorah, which he did. Oliver says that when Joseph and Oliver went there, the hill opened, and they walked into a cave, in which there was a large and spacious room. He says he did not think, at the time, whether they had the light of the sun or artificial light; but that it was just as light as day. They laid the plates on a table; it was a large table that stood in the room. Under this table there was a pile of plates as much as two feet high, and there were altogether in this room more plates than probably many wagon loads; they were piled up in the corners and along the walls. The first time they went there the sword of Laban hung upon the wall; but when they went again it had been taken down and laid upon the table across the gold plates; it was unsheathed, and on it was written these words: 'This sword will never be sheathed again until the kingdoms of this world become the kingdom of our God and his Christ.' I tell you this as coming not only from Oliver Cowdery, but others who were familiar with it, and who understand it just as well as we understand coming to this meeting . . . *I take this liberty of referring to those things so that they will not be forgotten and lost . . .*

"Now, you may think I am unwise in publicly telling these things, thinking perhaps I should preserve them in my own breast; but such is not my mind. *I would like the people called Latter-day Saints to understand some little things with regard to the workings and dealings of the Lord with his people here upon the earth.*" (*Journal of Discourses*, Volume 19, pp. 36-39; June 17, 1877. Italics added)

* * * * * *

ARTICLE TWELVE

The Brother of Jared's Chastening

In the Book of Mormon, the story of the brother of Jared is highly fascinating and spiritual. By his mighty faith, this blessed man was able to see and converse with the premortal Lord. Prior to this great manifestation, our Lord chastened this righteous man.

In the book of Ether, we read this account:

"And it came to pass at the end of four years that the Lord came again unto the brother of Jared, and stood in a cloud and talked with him. And for the space of three hours did the Lord talk with the brother of Jared, *and chastened him because he remembered not to call upon the name of the Lord.*" (2:14)

Over the years, and from many Saints, I have been taught that the brother of Jared was chastened by the Lord, for three hours, because for four years "he remembered not to call upon the name of the Lord."

Please allow me to present some truths that may be overlooked. What does it mean, "the Lord *came again* unto the brother of Jared?"

In chapter one, we read:

"And it came to pass that the brother of Jared did cry unto the Lord according to that which had been spoken by the mouth of Jared.

"And it came to pass that the Lord did hear the brother of Jared, and had compassion upon him, and *said unto him*: . . ." (1:39-40. Italics added)

The Lord actually spoke with the brother of Jared. Whether it was in his mind or vocally, we are left to wonder. In chapter two, we read of two times that the Lord stood in a cloud and verbally "talked" with him. (See verses 4 and 14)

To me, it seems inconsistent that if the brother of Jared ceased praying for the space of four years, why then does the Lord come "again" and verbally talk with him?

Continuing with verse fourteen, in chapter two: "And for the space of three hours did the Lord talk with the brother of Jared, and chastened him because he remembered not to call upon the name of the Lord."

One could infer from this verse that the Lord chastened him for three hours for not praying. However, please note where the comma is placed. A distinct separation is made from the Lord talking with the brother of Jared, and his chastening him. To me, it seems if the Lord solely chastened him for three hours for not praying, the scripture would read:

"And for the space of three hours did the Lord talk with the brother of Jared AND chastened him because he remembered not to call upon the Lord."

No comma would be between "Jared" and "and." Please allow me to present the information revealed in verses fifteen through sixteen.

"And the brother of Jared repented of the evil which he had done, and did call upon the name of the Lord *for his brethren who were with him:* . . ." (2:15. Italics added)

It seems to me that, the brother of Jared never stopped praying to the Lord; he committed a sin of omission by not praying "for his brethren who were with him."

Likewise, "his brethren" must not have prayed for the brother of Jared as well, for the Lord declares, "I will forgive thee *and thy brethren of their sins,* but thou shalt not sin any more . . ." (2:15. Italics added)

I believe the Lord not only chastened the brother of Jared for not praying "for his brethren," but, for "three hours," He was giving instructions on how to build the barges for the long journey upon the water. In support of this belief, the scripture reads:

"And the Lord said: Go to work and build, after the manner of barges which ye have hitherto built. And it came to pass that the brother of Jared did go to work, and also his brethren, and built barges after the manner which they had built,

according to the instructions of the Lord." (2:16.
Italics added)

The brother of Jared truly was a mighty prophet of
the Lord. May we study and pray about the sacred doctrines
revealed in the book of Ether.

* * * * *

ARTICLE THIRTEEN

Do Spirits Look
Like Mortals?

Do spirits resemble mortals in looks and appearance? The Lord has revealed that the premortal spirit that is housed in the mortal body is "in the likeness of that which is temporal." Let us read what is written:

> ". . . *that which is spiritual being in the likeness of that which is temporal*; and that which is temporal in the likeness of that which is spiritual; *the spirit of man in the likeness of his person*, as also the spirit of the beast, and every other creature which God has created." (D&C 77:2. Italics added)

Accordingly, all mortal beings take upon themselves physical characteristics that are similar to those of our premortal spirit. Regarding this doctrine, we read the words of Elder Orson Pratt:

> ". . . I believe that if our spirits could be taken from our bodies and stand before us, so that we could gaze upon them with our natural eyes, we would see *the likeness and image* of each of the tab-

ernacles out of which they were taken." (*Journal of Discourses*, Volume 2, p. 341; February 18, 1855)

In a latter address, he explains this about spirits:

"When we occupied our first estate, dwelling in the presence of the Father, . . . we were there as intelligent spirits, *in our present form and shape. . .*" (*Journal of Discourses*, Volume 19, p. 287; 1878)

With these comments, we turn our attention to an account in the Book of Mormon. Nearly six hundred years prior to the birth of Jesus Christ, the prophet Nephi was privileged to see what his father had seen in vision and obtained important information about the Spirit of the Lord:

"For it came to pass after I had desired to know the things that my father had seen, and believing that the Lord was able to make them known unto me, as I sat pondering in mine heart I was caught away in the Spirit of the Lord, yea, into an exceedingly high mountain, which I never had before seen, and upon which I never had before set my foot.

"And the Spirit said unto me: Behold, what desirest thou?

"And I said: I desire to behold the things which my father saw.

". . . for I spake unto him as a man speaketh; *for I beheld that he was in the form of a man*; yet nevertheless, *I knew that it was the Spirit of the Lord*; and he spake unto me as a man speaketh with another." (1 Ne.11: 1-3, 11. Italics added)

Brother of Jared's Experience

Now, we turn to the marvelous account recorded in the book of Ether where the brother of Jared sees the finger of the spirit Lord. We begin by reading a portion of his mighty prayer:

> "And I know, O Lord, that thou hast all power, and can do whatsoever thou wilt for the benefit of man; *therefore touch these stones*, O Lord, *with thy finger*, and prepare them that they may shine forth in darkness; and they shall shine forth unto us in the vessels which we have prepared, that we may have light while we shall cross the sea . . .
>
> "And it came to pass that when the brother of Jared had said these words, behold, the *Lord stretched forth his hand* and touched the stones one by one *with his finger*. And the veil was taken from off the eyes of the brother of Jared, and *he saw the finger of the Lord*; . . ."

Please note these next revealing words:

> "and it was **as the** *finger of a man*, **like unto flesh and blood**; and the brother of Jared fell down before the Lord, for he was struck with fear.
>
> "And the Lord saw that the brother of Jared had fallen to the earth; and the Lord said unto him:

Arise, why hast thou fallen?

"And he saith unto the Lord: *I saw the finger of the Lord*, and I feared lest he should smite me; **for I knew not that the Lord had flesh and blood.**

"And the Lord said unto him: *Because of thy faith thou hast seen that **I shall take upon me flesh and blood**; and never has man come before me with such *exceeding faith* as thou hast; for were it not so ye could not have seen my finger . . ." (Ether 3: 4-9. Italics and bold letters added)

Flesh And Blood

What does the expression *flesh and blood* mean? It refers to or means mortality (See Lev. 17: 11; Matt. 16: 16-17). Based on this knowledge, we return again to the account of the brother of Jared. We can properly assume that before this righteous man *"saw the finger of the Lord,"* he knew the doctrine that "God created man in his own image, in the image of God created he him; male and female created he them" (See Gen. 1: 27). In addition, the Spirit Lord had spoken to him three times previously (See Ether 1:40; 2:4, 14). Accordingly, this man knew that the Lord was able to speak and communicate as a man. Therefore, when the brother of Jared exclaimed, *"for I knew not that the Lord had flesh and blood,"* would it be unreasonable to believe that it had nothing to do with the form of our Savior, *but that he was surprised that our Lord's spirit finger had color or pigmentation the same as mortals?*

Regarding this experience of the brother of Jared,

we read these revealing words of Elder B. H. Roberts:

"We read of Jesus, the Christ, appearing unto Moriancumer upon the mount; and when by faith Moriancumer saw the finger of that spirit he pleaded that he might have a full vision of the divine personage of the Christ. The veil parted and the Christ, his pre-existent spirit, stood before the prophet, and said to him: 'Behold, this body, which ye now behold, is the body of my spirit; . . . and even as I appear unto thee to be in the spirit will I appear unto my people in the flesh.' From this we gather the fact that it is *the expression of the spirit that shines through the tabernacle; that if spirit and body could be separated and placed side by side, we would see then that the inner man had fashioned after his own likeness the outward man* . . . So that character, the nobility of it, the greatness and goodness of it in any individual case *depends upon what the pre-existent spirit was*—that is, what the spirit was before it tabernacled in the flesh."

Though science teaches that we inherit our appearances and character traits from our parents and grandparents, Elder Roberts reveals this about heredity:

"***It is to the spirits of men,*** *then,* ***that you want to look for the determining factor of character rather than to earthly parentage—rather than to heredity*** . . . So, I repeat, it is with the *Spirits of men* that we have to deal rather than with *heredity*. (An Address, June 11, 1916, printed in *Young Women's Journal*, Volume 27, pp. 524-530; September, 1916. Italics and bold letters added)

Regarding spirits, especially those of infants, we turn to the expressions of Elder Orson Pratt:

"Let us enquire, for a few moments, concerning the nature of these spiritual bodies which are thus restored back into the presence of God. A great many people have supposed that the spirit which exists in the tabernacle, for instance, of an infant, is of the same size as the infant tabernacle when it enters therein. No one will dispute that it is of the same size when it is enclosed therein; *but how large was the spirit before it entered the tabernacle? Was it a full grown male or female spirit, or was it a little infant spirit in its pre-existent state?*"

He then specifically uses the experience of the brother of Jared to explain the size of premortal spirits.

". . . for if we turn to the Book of Ether we shall find that the Lord Jesus, who was one of these spirits, and the first-born of the whole family, *was a personage like unto a man, without flesh, blood or bones, but a full-grown spirit*, thousands of years before he came to take his infant tabernacle. Is it so recorded in the Book of Ether? Yes . . . .

". . . *Behold, this body which you now see is*

*the body of my spirit, and all men in the beginning
have I created after the body of my spirit.'* . . . [See
Ether 3:16]

"When all these spirits were sent forth from
the eternal worlds, they were, no doubt, *not infants*;
but when they entered this infant tabernacle, they
were under the necessity, the same as our Lord and
Savior, of being *compressed, or diminished in size
so that their spirits could be enclosed in infant tabernacles.*"

He then asks and answers this intriguing question:

"If their bodies die in infancy, do their spirits
remain infants in stature between death and the resurrection of the body? I think not. Why not?
Because the redemption must restore everything to
its natural order . . ." (*Journal of Discourses*,
Volume 16, pp. 333-335; Dec. 28, 1873. Italics
added)

Spirit And Physical Growth

Regarding the spirit and how it affects the growth
and size of the physical body it is temporarily housed in, we
rely once again upon the wisdom of Elder Orson Pratt:

"The tabernacles of both animals and vegeta-
bles continue to grow or increase in size, until they
attain to the original magnitude of their respective
spirits, after which the growth ceases. When the

spirit first takes possession of the vegetable or animal seed or embryo, it contracts itself into a bulk of
the same dimension as the seed or tabernacle into
which it enters: . . . Spirits, therefore, must be composed of substances, highly elastic in their nature,
that is, they have the power to resume their former
dimensions, as additional matter is secreted for the
enlargement of their tabernacles. It is this expand-
ing force, exerted by the spirit, which gradually
develops the tabernacle as the necessary materials
are supplied." (*The Seer*, Washington D.C. Edition,
March, 1853; p.36)

It is apparent that the spirit is quite elastic. The spirit leaves the premortal estate as a full grown entity, and
upon entering the seed or physical body, it "contracts" to
the size of the person, animal, or plant. Then, through a
period of mortal months or years, attains to the physical
height the spirit had reached in the premortal life.

Spirit And Physical Deformities

Regarding physical deformities and disfigurements
manifested in mortality, and their relationship to the spirit
housed in the tabernacle, we use the wisdom of Elders Pratt
and Talmage:

"We, as Latter-day Saints, believe that the
spirits that occupy these tabernacles have form and
likeness similar to the human tabernacle. Of course
there may be deformities existing in connection with

the outward tabernacle which do not exist in connection with the spirit that inhabits it. These tabernacles become deformed by accident in various ways, sometimes at birth, but this may not altogether or in any degree deform the spirits that dwell within them, therefore we believe that the spirits which occupy the bodies of the human family are more or less in the resemblance of the tabernacles." (Orson Pratt, *Journal of Discourses*, Volume 15, pp. 242.243; Dec. 15, 1872)

In addition to this expression, we read these inspired words from Elder Talmage:

"We know but little of things beyond the sphere upon which we live except as information has been revealed by a power superior to that of earth, and by an intelligence above that of man. Notwithstanding the assumption that man is the culmination of an evolutionary development from a lower order of beings, we know that the body of man today is in the very form and fashion of his spirit, except indeed for disfigurements and deformities. The perfect body is the counterpart of the perfect spirit and the two are the constituent entities of the soul." (James E. Talmage, Council of the Twelve, An address delivered in the Tabernacle in Salt Lake City, Utah, August 9, 1931, entitled *The Earth and Man*. Reprint from the *Deseret News*, November 21, 1931. Also recorded in the *Millennial Star*, 93: 853-854, December 31, 1931)

Therefore, we can determine that physical deformities have no real correlation between the spirit and the physical body. To support this teaching, especially as it pertains to the resurrection of the body and the spirit, the scripture reveals:

> *"The spirit and the body shall be reunited again in its perfect form; both limb and joint shall be restored to its proper frame . . .*
>
> "Now, this restoration shall come to all, both old and young, . . . both male and female . . . *and even there shall not so much as a hair of their heads be lost; but every thing shall be restored to its perfect frame . . ."* (Alma 11: 43-44. Italics added)

Other than physical deformities, we now know that the premortal spirit that is housed in the mortal body is *"in the likeness of that which is temporal."* Then, what is this likeness? It is this: If we could see our spirit bodies standing by our sides, we would see that they have the same look, are the same size, have the same shape, and have the same identities. To support this doctrine, the Lord has revealed, *". . . the spirit of man in the likeness of his person."* (D&C 77: 2. Italics added)

* * * * * *

ARTICLE FOURTEEN

Spiritual Fluid

Regarding our resurrected Lord, President Brigham Young gives this insightful information:

> "The blood he [Jesus Christ] spilled upon Mount Calvary he did not receive again into his veins. That was poured out, and when he was resurrected, *another element took the place of the blood.* It will be so with every person who receives a resurrection: the blood will not be resurrected with the body, being designed only to sustain the life of the present organization." (*Journal of Discourses,* Volume 7, p. 163; June 5, 1859. Italics added)

Therefore, it is proper to ask, After the resurrection, what is this "*element*" that takes the place of blood? To help answer this intriguing question, we read these revealing words of Charles W. Penrose, who was ordained an apostle on July 7, 1904, and later became a counselor in the First Presidency:

> THE RESURRECTION: "The corruptible blood was purged from the veins [of Jesus Christ],

and *incorruptible spiritual fluid occupied its place. It was buried a natural body, it was resurrected a spiritual body.*" ("Mormon" Doctrine, Plain and Simple, or, Leaves from the Tree of Life. Published 1888, p. 44. Italics added)

Comparing the difference between blood and this "incorruptible spiritual fluid," we read these comments by Elder Orson Pratt:

"Blood, instead of imparting eternal life to the system, only imparts a natural or temporal life, and contains within itself all the ingredients of decay and death or dissolution."

Specifically speaking of Adam and Eve, before mortality entered the world, we read these interesting suppositions:

"It is reasonable to suppose, then, that *a fluid of a more refined and life-giving nature,* flowed through the bodily organizations of our first Parents, and all other animal creation—that *this fluid was the life-preserving agent, that imparted immortality to all flesh,* so long as they retained it in their systems. As this fluid could not have been blood which contains the seeds of death, What kind of substance was it? We reply, that it must have been a *spiritual substance or fluid,* which is the only kind of substance capable of preserving any organization in immortality." (*The Seer,* Washington D.C. Edition, March, 1853; p.70. Italics added)

Blood And Spiritual Fluid

How then is "*blood*" and "*spiritual fluid*" created? Again, we rely upon the interesting understanding of Elder Orson Pratt:

> "The celestial vegetables and fruits which grow out of the soil of this redeemed Heaven, constitute the food of the Gods. This food differs from the food derived from the vegetables of a fallen world; the latter are converted into *blood*, which, circulating in the veins and arteries, produces flesh and bones of a mortal nature, having a constant tendency to decay; while the former, or celestial vegetables, are, when digested in the stomach, *converted into a fluid*, which, in its nature, *is spiritual*, and which, circulating in the veins and arteries of the celestial male and female, preserves their tabernacles from decay and death. *Earthly vegetables form blood*, and blood forms flesh and bones; *celestial vegetables*, when digested, *form a spiritual fluid* which gives immortality and eternal life to the organization in which it flows." (Ibid., p. 37. Italics added)

Whether or not we eat in the hereafter is an intriguing topic. This article will not address this subject. Now, comparing blood and spiritual fluid, we obtain this revealing information about offspring from Elder Melvin J. Ballard:

"The nature of the offspring is determined by the nature of the substance that flows in the veins of the being. When blood flows in the veins of the being, the offspring will be what blood produces, which is tangible flesh and bone, but when that which flows in the veins is spirit matter, a substance which is more refined and pure and glorious than blood, the offspring of such beings will be spirit children." (*The Three Degrees of Glory*, A discourse given at the Ogden Tabernacle, September 22, 1922, p. 10)

Because God the Father does not have blood running through his resurrected body, *but spirit matter or spiritual fluid*, the number of people who have lived or will yet live upon this earth are his spirit children.

The Mortal Jesus Christ

The fluid that is circulated through human beings is called blood. Blood being more heavy than spirit matter, we know that this is the predominant element in determining what type of offspring the premortal Christ would become in mortality.

From this information, we can more fully understand why Mary, who is a mortal being with blood flowing in her veins, is overshadowed by the Highest, an immortal being with "spirit matter" or "spiritual fluid" flowing through his veins, and that holy child of their sacred union will become the mortal Jesus Christ, with both fluids flowing in his veins. From his mother, our Lord inherits the ability to die physically because of the blood; from his Father, Christ inherits the power to live forever because of spiritual fluid. We know that when Jesus died on the cross, he said, "Father, into thy hands I commend my spirit: and having said thus, he [voluntarily] gave up the ghost." (Luke 23:46)

Conclusion

From what has been revealed, we know that mortals have *blood* flowing in their veins, which "only imparts a natural or temporal life, and contains within itself all the ingredients of decay and death or dissolution." Then, after the "resurrection, another element" will take the place of the blood. This element is referred to as "spirit matter" or "a spiritual substance or fluid, which is the only kind of substance capable of preserving any organization in immortality."

* * * * * *

ARTICLE FIFTEEN

Age Of The Earth
(Part One)

Eternal Duration Of Matter

The age of the earth and the universe are mysteries that have caused many individuals to wonder how to correlate the truths of religion with the truths of science. Let us discover what religious truths have been revealed on this intriguing subject. From the Old Testament, we read these simple but meaningful words:

> "In the beginning God created the heaven and the earth.
> "And the earth was without form, and void;..." (Gen. 1:1-2. See also Moses 2:1-2; Abr. 3:1-2)

Meaning Of The Word "Create"

Based on this information, it is proper to ask, How did God create the heaven and the earth? To help answer this question, we turn to the Prophet Joseph Smith for understanding:

"You ask the learned doctors why they say the world was made out of nothing; and they will answer, 'Doesn't the Bible say He *created* the world?' And they infer, from the word create, that it must have been made out of nothing. Now, the word *create* came from the word *baurau* which does not mean to *create out of nothing*; it means to *organize*; the same as a man would organize materials and build a ship. Hence, we infer that God had materials to organize the world out of chaos—chaotic *matter*, *which is element*, and in which dwells all the glory. Element had an existence from the time he had. *The pure principles of element are principles which can never be destroyed; they may be organized and re-organized, but not destroyed. They had no beginning, and can have no end.*" (*Journal of Discourses*, Volume 6, p. 6; April 6, 1844. Wording from *Teachings of the Prophet Joseph Smith*, pp. 350-352. Italics added)

President George Q. Cannon

Regarding this particular teaching, we read these insightful words of President George Q. Cannon, who was a counselor in the First Presidency:

"Another step has been made in advance, through the preaching of the Elders of this Church, or rather by means of the revelations of God through the Prophet Joseph Smith, *in scientific truth which is astonishing*; I refer to the *doctrine of the eternal duration of matter.* When first this was made known it was ridiculed everywhere by religious people, who viewed it as a principle, the teachings of which detracted from the dignity and glory of God. The popular idea was that this earth was created out of nothing. This was the almost universal belief among Christians. Joseph Smith said it was not true. *He advocated the doctrine that matter always had an existence, that it was eternal as God Himself was eternal; that it was indestructible; that it never had a beginning, and therefore could have no end.* God revealed this truth to him. Now who is there that does not believe it?

"So with regard to the periods occupied in the creation of the earth[,] Joseph taught that a day with God was not the twenty-four hours of our day; but that the six days of the creation were six periods of the Lord's time."

President Cannon then gives this interesting observation:

"This he taught half a century ago; it is now generally received as a great truth connected with the creation of the world. Geologists have declared it, and religious people are adopting it; and so the world is progressing." (*Journal of Discourses,* Volume 24, p. 61; March 18, 1883. Italics added)

Matter

Regarding "matter, which is element," we read these interesting words from President Brigham Young:

> "There is not a particle of element which is not filled with life, and all space is filled with element; there is no such thing as empty space, though some philosophers contend that there is."

Regarding forms of matter, he gives specific examples:

> "There is life in all matter, throughout the vast extent of all the eternities; it is in the rock, the sand, the dust, in water, air, the gases, and, in short, in every description and organization of matter, whether it be solid, liquid, or gaseous, particle operating with particle . . .
>
> "True, element is capable of contraction and expansion but that does not by any means imply empty spaces. You see life in human beings and in the growing vegetation, and when that spirit of life departs, another condition of life at once begins to operate upon the organization which remains." (*Journal of Discourses*, Volume 3, p. 277; March 23, 1856)

In an earlier address, he explains how matter still exists though it may change its original form:

"In the first place, matter is eternal. The principle of annihilation, of striking out of existence anything that has existed, or had a being, so as to leave an empty space which that thing occupied, is false, there is no such principle in all the *eternities*. [He asks this question:] What does exist? [He then uses logic and wisdom to answer his own question:] Matter is eternal. We grow our wheat, our fruit, and our animals, [sic—the comma instead of a period.] There they are organized, they increase and grow; but, after a while, they decay, dissolve, become disorganized, and return to their mother earth. No matter by what process, these are the revolutions which they undergo; *but the elements of the particles of which they were composed, still do, always have, and always will exist*, and through this principle of change, we have an eternal increase."

Eternal Organization Used
By The Lord

Speaking specifically of our Savior, President Young reveals this unique doctrine:

"The Lord operates upon the principles of continuing to organize, of adding to, gathering up, bringing forth, increasing and spreading abroad. . ." (*Journal of Discourses*, Volume 1, pp. 116-117; February 27, 1853. Italics added)

Regarding this statement, both the Father and the Son are continually using this eternal law and truth:

"For behold, this is my work and my glory—to bring to pass the immortality and eternal life of man" (Moses 1:39). In support of this doctrine, we read these revealing words:

"And worlds without number have I created...and by the Son I created them, which is mine Only Begotten." (Ibid., v. 33)

These supreme beings are continually organizing worlds and bringing forth children to populate them. And for what reason? As it pertains to our earth—as well as others—we turn to the book of Abraham for the answer:

Why Our Earth Was Created

In the Pearl of Great Price, we read:

"Now the Lord had shown unto me, Abraham, the intelligences that were organized before the world was; and among all these there were many of the noble and great ones . . .

"And there stood one among them that was like unto God, and he said unto those who were with him: We will go down, for there is space there, and we will take of these materials, *and we will make an earth whereon these may dwell* . . .

"And we will prove them herewith, to see if they will do all things whatsoever the Lord their God shall command them;

"... and they who keep their second estate shall have glory added upon their heads for ever and ever.

"And then the Lord said: Let us go down. And they went down at the beginning, *and they, that is the Gods, organized and formed the heavens and the earth.* (Abraham 3:22; 24-26; 4:1. Italics added)

Speaking specifically of the earth that we live on, we read these declarative words of President Young:

"Latter-day Saints . . . believe God brought forth *material* out of which he formed this little *terra firma* upon which we roam. *How long had this material been in existence? Forever and forever, in some shape, in some condition.*" (*Journal of Discourses*, Volume 18, p. 232; September 17, 1876. Italics added)

Elder Orson Pratt

Regarding the "material" that formed this earth, we turn to the expressions of Elder Orson Pratt:

"If we had the process of creation unfolded to us, we should probably find that many of the *materials* of our globe once existed in a dispersed or scattered form, in a state of chaos, and that the Lord, in collecting them together, brought them from a distance in the solar system, and that in so doing, he took his own time and way, and wrought according to his own laws, for, as far as we are acquainted, the Lord works by law, and why not create by law? I do not mean out of nothing

. . . The work of creation was to take the *materials* that existed from all eternity, that never were created or made out of nothing, to take these self-existent materials and organize them into a world. This is called creation." (*Journal of Discourses*, Volume 16, p. 315; November 22, 1873. Italics added)

From these various expressions, we understand that God formed our earth out of matter or material that "*may be organized and re-organized, but not destroyed.*" Further, that there is life in all matter, throughout the vast extent of all the eternities, whether it be solid, liquid, or gaseous, particle operating with particle.

A Meaning For The Word "Day"

Again from Elder Orson Pratt, we read these informative words about the word "day" or "days":

"We know, according to the declaration of the Scriptures, that our earth was made some few thousands years ago. How long the progress of formation lasted we do not know. It is called in the Scriptures six days; but we do not know the meaning of the scriptural term *day*. It evidently does not mean such days as we are now acquainted with—

days governed by the rotation of the earth on its axis, and by the shining of the great central luminary of our solar system. **A day of twenty-four hours is not the kind of day referred to in the scriptural account of the creation.**"

He then uses specific examples to emphasize his point.

". . . the word *days*, in the Scriptures, seems oftentimes to refer to some indefinite period of time. The Lord, in speaking to Adam in the garden says, 'In the day that thou eatest thereof thou shalt surely die'; [See Gen. 2: 17] *yet he did not die within twenty-four hours after he had eaten the forbidden fruit*, but he lived to be almost a thousand years old, [He died when he was 930 years old—See Gen. 5:5] from which we learn that the word *day*, in this passage, had no reference to days of the same duration as ours. Again, it is written, in the second chapter of Genesis, 'In the *day* that He created the heavens and the earth' [See verse 4]; not six days, but, 'in the *day*' that he did it, incorporating all the six days into one, and calling that period 'the *day*' that He created the heavens and the earth."

He then concludes by stating how long it took the earth to be formed:

"But however long or short may have been the period of the construction of this earth, we find that *some six thousand years ago it seems to have been formed*, something after the fashion and in the manner in which it now exists, with the exception of the imperfections, evils, and curses that exist on the face of it." (*Journal of Discourses*, Volume 14, pp. 234-235; August 20, 1871. Italics added)

Age Of The Earth

Regarding the age of the earth, we read these interesting expressions of President Brigham Young:

"You take, for instance, our geologists, and they tell us that this earth has been in existence for thousands and millions of years. They think . . . that their researches and investigations enable them to demonstrate that this earth has been in existence as long as they assert it has . . .

"You may take geology, for instance, and it is a true science; not that I would say for a moment that all the conclusions and deductions of its professors are true, but its leading principles are . . . that the Lord made this earth out of nothing is preposterous and impossible. God never made something out of nothing; it is not in the economy or law by which the worlds were, are, or will exist. There is an eternity before us, and it is full of matter; and if we but understand enough of the Lord and his ways, we would say that he took of this matter and organized this earth from it. How long it has been organized it is not for me to say, and I do not care anything about it . . .

"If we understood the process of creation there would be no mystery about it, it would be all reasonable and plain, for there is no mystery except to the ignorant." (*Journal of Discourses*, Volume 14, pp. 115-116; May 14, 1871. Italics added)

From these various expressions, we know that matter has always been in existence, and that the Gods formed our earth from this eternal element. Next, we will learn how long it took to create the earth.

ARTICLE SIXTEEN

Age Of The Earth
(Part Two)

Creation Of The Earth
Is Based On Days

From the Lord, as well as his servants, we find out that the creation of the earth is based on days. In addition, that these days were based on Kolob time.

Kolob

We read this interesting information about Kolob from Elder Orson Pratt:

"These *six days* in which the Lord performed this work, I do not believe, were each limited to twenty-four hours, as are the periods which we now call *day*; indeed, *when we come to new revelation, we find some light on this subject.* In the Book of Abraham, as well as in the inspired translation of the Scriptures, given through Joseph Smith, the Lord says, in speaking of the work of creating this earth, that he was governed by celestial time. According to this new revelation, there is a certain great world, called *Kolob*, placed near one of the celestial kingdoms, whose diurnal rotation takes place *once in a thousand of our years*; and that celestial time was measured by those celestial beings, by the rotations of Kolob, *hence one day with the Lord was a thousand of our years* [See Abraham 3: 4, 9]. If this was the case, *the six days of the creation of our earth, the six days during which it was being prepared as a habitation for man, must have been six thousand of our years.*" (*Journal of Discourses*, Volume 16, p. 317; November 22, 1873. Italics added. See also Joseph Fielding Smith, *Doctrines of Salvation*, Volume 1, pp. 78-81)

Elder Erastus Snow

Using logic and wisdom, Elder Erastus Snow explains this about the creation of the earth:

"We read in this first chapter of Genesis, that in six days the Lord created the heavens and the earth. Now modern scientists attempt to confute [to disprove] this history given by Moses, by demonstrating that the earth has been formed through the operation of a long process of natural laws, and that it never could be brought into its present condition in six days. Of course, those who reason thus assume that the days here spoken of were periods of the same duration as the days counted out to us by the revolution of the earth on its axis, every time it turns upon its axis and marks the day and night. But I must be allowed to call attention to this one fact, that in the beginning of this history Moses tells us that when God first organized or created the elements of the earth, that it was without form and void; that is to say it was without its present form, and that darkness was upon the face of the abyss."

He then asks and answers this intriguing question:

"Then how were the days reckoned? . . .

"Philosophers and astronomers have not lived long enough upon this earth, or kept a record of the heavenly bodies long enough to make any calculation of the length of this period. There is, however, one saying of Apostle Peter which reads—'Be not ignorant of this one thing, that one day is with the Lord as a thousand years, and a thousand years as one day' [See 2 Peter 3:8]. But whether that has any reference to the days that Moses speaks of, in which the Lord was engaged in the formation of this earth, we are not told. But be the periods longer or shorter, which the Lord called *six periods, or days*, in which he did his work, is of very little importance to us. [He then gives some sound advice.] *Nor is it worth our time to question or contend with geologists or modern scientist as to the duration of these periods*. It is a fact that the earth exists, and that it has its sphere in which it moves, and that it is appointed for the abode of man, and that we are here, and the fathers have told us we have descended from the Gods."

Next, he gives advice to those who believe in the scientific point of view:

"... the creation is a reality. We see a variety of solid rocks, and ask, How are they formed? Geologists undertake to tell us, and they refer us to the Book of Nature. But they are like other school children; *they make a great many mistakes in reading*. What they read correctly is correct; what they read incorrectly is incorrect. [He then uses a little, humorous saying to emphasize his point:] 'It is as it is, and it can't be any tisser.'[sic] *And it is folly for geologists, or any other class of scientists, to assume that they know it all*, or that they have read the Book of Nature from beginning to end, and comprehend it through and through."

Regarding the creation, he presents these thought-provoking comments:

"This house, in which we meet, when was this created? Oh, about 15 or 20 years ago. Still the philosophers will tell you that the trees from which the lumber was sawn, must have been hundreds of years old. Oh, to tell me that this house was made only 15 or 20 years ago, I know better; my knowledge of timber teaches me that the very trees from which the lumber war [sic—should be "was"], were several hundred years old. And the geologist will take you to the hills or along the beach and point out to you the evidences in nature of the long periods that must have elapsed since the formation of the sedimentary rocks, to say nothing about the primary rocks. And they will tell you that the period alluded to in Moses, in the history of Adam, and to the creation is scarcely a cypher [sic] compared with the period in which these elements of the earth have been coming into shape. What is all that to do with the great grand principle[?] We will say that the component parts of every implement formed by the ingenuity and labor of man are far older than the implement itself." (*Journal of Discourses*, Volume 19:324-327; January 20, 1878. Italics added)

From these words, we know that the "materials" that made this earth are much older than the earth itself. Next, we will learn about the temporal existence of the earth.

* * * * * *

ARTICLE SEVENTEEN

Age Of The Earth
(Part Three)

Temporal Existence Of The Earth

Now, let us turn our attention to the time of the temporal existence of the earth. From the Bible, in the book of Revelation, we read of the opening of seven seals by the Lamb of God, and each seal represents a thousand years of temporal existence of the earth (See Chapters five through nine). In support of this time-frame, we read about these seals in the Doctrine and Covenants (See section 88: 92-116—especially verses 101 and 110 which read a "thousand years"). In section 77 of the Doctrine and Covenants, we receive more information about opening these seals, with a specific time mentioned:

> "Q. What are we to understand by the book which John saw, which was sealed on the back with seven seals?
>
> "A. We are to understand that it contains the revealed will, mysteries, and the works of God; the hidden things of his economy *concerning this earth during the **seven thousand years of its contin-***

*uance, or **its temporal existence**.*" (verse 6. Italics and boldface added)

In this same section of the Doctrine and Covenants, we read these marvelous and clarifying words about the creation and temporal existence of this earth:

"We are to understand that as God *made the world in six days*, and on *the seventh day he finished his work*, and sanctified it, and also formed man out of the dust of the earth . . ." (verse 12. Italics added)

From the Lord himself, we read that the *creation process* took six days, or six thousand years, and he finished his work on the seventh day, thereby, making the total creation process seven thousand years. Again, we continue with this particular revelation about the temporal existence of the earth:

". . . *in the beginning of the seventh thousand years will the Lord God sanctify the earth*, and complete the salvation of man, and judge all things, and shall redeem all things . . . *in the beginning of the seventh thousand years*—the preparing of the way before the time of his coming." (verse 12. Italics added)

This pertains to the millennium, when the Lord will once again come to the earth. In light of this, it is proper to wonder when the Lord was born on the earth. To answer, we learn the meaning of the words *meridian of time*.

Meridian Of Time

As it pertains to the age of the earth, we know that the Lord came in the meridian of time (See Moses 5:57; D&C 20: 26). This means that it was about halfway from the fall and the end of the temporal existence of the earth. (See also Joseph Fielding Smith, *Doctrines of Salvation*, Volume 1, p. 81)

Millennium Time Near

We know that The Church of Jesus Christ of Latter-day Saints was organized "one thousand eight hundred and thirty years since the coming of our Lord and Savior Jesus Christ in the flesh" (See D&C 20: 1). We know that *"in the beginning of the seventh thousand years will the Lord God sanctify the earth*, and complete the salvation of man, and judge all things, and shall redeem all things" (D&C 77:12). Further, He shall personally reign over and visit the earth during this time. (See Article of Faith 10; see also, *Teachings of the Prophet Joseph Smith*, p. 268) Whether the millennium will be ten or a hundred years after the year 2000, we know that the time is near. (See Bruce R. McConkie, *A New Witness for the Articles of Faith*, p. 636)

Satan Loosed For A Season

During the millennium, Satan will be bound and not be able to tempt individuals. However, after this thousand years of peace, he will be loosed for a *little season* (See Rev. 6: 11; 20: 1-3; D&C 29: 22; D&C 88: 110-111). It has been written that "perhaps" this "little season" is also a thousand years. (See Bruce R. McConkie, *A New Witness for the Articles of Faith*, p.651)

Summation About The Earth's Existence

We have discovered from the Prophet Joseph Smith, and other Church leaders, that God brought forth *material out of which he formed this earth, and that this matter has been in existence forever, in some shape, and in some condition.* Therefore, from what Elder Snow has stated, "that the component parts of every implement formed by the ingenuity and labor of man [and may we add God also] are far older than the implement itself," it seems reasonable to believe that the materials that formed this earth are more than six thousand years old; however, the actual creation process only involved six days of the Lord's time, which total six thousand years. Then, he finished his work on the seventh day, which was another thousand years. Besides the creation process, we know that this earth has gone through six thousand years of temporal existence; thereby making this earth about thirteen thousand years old (See also Joseph Fielding Smith, *Doctrines of Salvation*, Volume 1, pp. 78-81). Next, we will learn about the age of the universe.

* * * * * *

ARTICLE EIGHTEEN

Age Of The Universe

In conjunction with the age of the earth, it is proper to wonder about the age of the universe that surrounds our earth. Are they the same age or are they different? Let us find out what has been revealed on this intriguing question.

From the Prophet Joseph Smith, we discover that a Mr. Michael H. Chandler inherited some mummies and rolls of papyrus from his deceased uncle, who found the artifacts in one of the catacombs in Egypt. Through the providence of the Lord, some members of the Church purchased these items, and gave them to the Prophet Joseph. When he began to translate them, he was delighted to find that one of the papyrus contained the writings of Abraham and the other, the writings of Joseph of Egypt.

W. W. Phelps and Oliver Cowdery acted as scribes during the translation of the ancient hieroglyphics (See *History of the Church*, Volume 2, pp. 235-236; 348-351. See also heading of The Book of Abraham in the *Pearl of Great Price*). From another writing, it is learned that W. W. Phelps was the secretary to the Prophet Joseph Smith during the translation of the papyrus. (An Examination of Science and the Religion of the Latter-day Saints, A Textbook Prepared for the Course Theology 325, B.Y.U. Press, 1958, p. 109)

In the *Times and Seasons*, an earlier publication of the Church, William W. Phelps is quoted as saying:

"Well, now, Brother William [Smith], when the house of Israel begin to come into the glorious mysteries of the kingdom, *and find that Jesus Christ, whose goings forth*, as the prophets said, have been from of old, from eternity: *and that eternity, agreeably to the records found in the catacombs of Egypt*, [from one of the papyrus found with the mummies] has been going on in this system, (not this world) [sic] ***almost two thousand five hundred and fifty five millions of years***: and to know at the same time, that deists, geologists and others are trying to prove that ***matter*** must have existed hundreds of thousands of years;—it almost tempts the flesh to fly to God, or muster faith like Enoch to be translated and see and know as we are seen and known!" (5:758; December 25, 1844. Italics and boldface added)

Evidently, in 1844, the word "billion" was not widely used. (The word "billion" was listed in Noah Webster's 1828 edition of the American Dictionary of the English Language.) When the year is written out numerically it is 2,555,000,000. In a written work by Elder Bruce R.

McConkie, he interprets Brother Phelps' calculation as not only applying to the system or universe that we live in, but to the time our Savior—as well as all of us—lived in the pre-mortal life, preparing to come to this earth. (See *The Mortal Messiah: From Bethlehem to Calvary, Book* 1, pp. 29-33, 315)

Accordingly, the age of the earth and the age of the universe are not the same. The age of our universe, which presumably calculates the time when God the Father became our God, is 2,555,000,000 years old.

* * * * * *

ARTICLE NINETEEN

Urim And Thummim
And
Seer Stone

One of the most intriguing mysteries of the gospel is the seer stone and its relationship to the Urim and Thummim. We know that the Prophet Joseph had a seer stone, but for what reason, we are not fully informed. Therefore, let us learn what has been written on this interesting subject.

Urim And Thummim

From the scriptures, we know that there have been more than one Urim and Thummim. We know that Abraham had one (See Abra. 3: 1-4). From the Bible, we learn that Aaron had one and it was handed down from generation to generation (See Ex. 28:30; Lev. 8:8; Num. 27:21; Deut. 33:8; 1 Sam. 28:6; Ezra 2:63; and Neh. 7:65). From the Book of Mormon, we know that the brother of Jared had one. (Ether 3:22-24, 27-28) We will learn later that Mosiah also used this instrument to translate.

Interpreters

Regarding these different *"interpreters"* (See Mosiah 8:13-17), we turn to President George Q. Cannon, of the First Presidency, for explanation:

"Questions have arisen in a Sunday School in one of the country wards in regard to the Urim and Thummim that was found with the plates of the Book of Mormon which the Prophet Joseph Smith received. The question appears to be, (*as this Urim and Thummim received by Joseph was the instrument given to the brother of Jared,*) has there ever been more than one of these entrusted to man on the earth at the same time? The Israelites in the days of Aaron had the Urim and Thummim; is this the same Urim and Thummim that was handed down from the Jaredites? If it is, how did it get from the Jaredites to the children of Israel, and from the children of Israel to the Nephites?

[His Answer:] "There is no record of such a transmission of the Urim and Thummim from one continent to another. It is in the highest degree improbable that the Urim and Thummim that the Jaredites had was the same that was had among the children of Israel. *It seems entirely clear that the Jaredites, and after them the Nephites, had the Urim and Thummim that the brother of Jared used,* and that the Urim and Thummim used among the children of Israel was one that had been prepared for use among them. The continent of America, as we now call it, was as though it were a distinct world, so far as the other hemisphere was concerned. Its existence was unknown. There was no connection between the people that dwelt on this land and the people that dwelt on the other continents. While, therefore, it is but reasonable to assume that the Lord permits the use of but one Urim and Thummim at a time on the earth, in the case of the Jaredites and Nephites such a rule might not apply, because, as we have said, they were as widely separated from the rest of the world and as unknown to those who lived on the eastern hemisphere as if they dwelt on a different planet." (*The Juvenile Instructor* 32:52; January 15, 1897. Italics added) [For a similar explanation, see Joseph Fielding Smith, *Doctrines of Salvation*, Volume 3, p. 222]

Joseph's Urim And Thummim

We know that Joseph's Urim and Thummim was the same one used by the brother of Jared. From a revelation given through the Prophet, by the means of the Urim and Thummim, to Oliver Cowdery, David Whitmer, and Martin Harris, we read these marvelous words:

"Behold, I say unto you, that you must rely upon my word, which if you do with full purpose of heart, *you shall have a view of the plates, and also of the breastplate, the sword of Laban, the **Urim and Thummim, which were given to the***

brother of Jared upon the mount, when he talked with the Lord face to face, and the miraculous directors [Liahona—See 1 Nephi 16:10; Alma 37:38] which were given to Lehi while in the wilderness, on the borders of the Red Sea." (D& C 17:1. Italics and boldface added)

Therefore, the Urim and Thummim which the Prophet had was the one that was given to the brother of Jared (See Ether 3:23). This same instrument was also entrusted to the care of Mosiah, then to Alma, the son of Alma, and eventually it was hidden by an unidentified person in the Hill Cumorah. (See Mosiah 8:13-19; 28:13-20)

Urim And Thummim
Description

From the book of Ether, we read what the Lord tells the brother of Jared:

"And behold, these *two stones* will I give unto thee, and ye shall seal them up also with the things which ye shall write.

". . . wherefore I will cause in my own due time that these *stones shall magnify to the eyes of men these things which ye shall write* . . ." (Ether 3:23-24; Italics added). From the Old Testament, we read that they were usually carried in a breastplate over the heart (See Exodus 28:30; Leviticus 8:8). From the Book of Mormon, we learn that King Mosiah translated various plates "by the means of those *two stones which were fastened into the two rims of a bow*." (Mosiah 28:13. Italics added) From the Prophet Joseph Smith, we obtain this revealing information:

"He [the Angel Moroni] said there was a *book* deposited, *written upon gold plates,* giving an account of the former inhabitants of this continent, and the source from whence they sprang. He also said that the *fullness of the everlasting Gospel was contained in it,* as delivered *by the Savior to the ancient inhabitants*;

"Also, that there were *two stones in silver bows*—and these stones, *fastened to a breastplate, constituted what is called the Urim and Thummim*—deposited with the *plates*; and the possession and use of these stones were what constituted '*seers*' in ancient or former times; *and that God had prepared them for the purpose of translating the book.*" (*Joseph Smith—History* 1:34-35. Italics added)

Elder Parley P. Pratt

From Elder Parley P. Pratt, we gain this insight:

"With the records was found a curious instrument, called by the ancients the *Urim and Thummim*, which consisted of *two transparent stones, clear as crystal, set in the two rims of a bow*. This was in use in ancient times by persons called *seers*. It was an instrument by the use of which they received revelation of things distant, or of things past or future." (*Voice of Warning*, p. 92; 1837. Italics added)

Meaning Of Urim And Thummim

According to the Bible Dictionary, the Urim and Thummim is a Hebrew term that means *Lights* and *Perfections*. Based on this information, it is safe to believe that of these "two stones," one is called *Urim* and the other is called *Thummim*.

Items With The Gold Plates

In the Prophet's own words, we read what was with the plates:

"At length the time arrived for obtaining the plates, the *Urim and Thummim*, and the breastplate. On the twenty-second day of September, one thousand eight hundred and twenty-seven . . ." (*Joseph Smith—History* 1:59. Italics added)

Information About
A Seer Stone

From President Brigham Young, we acquire this interesting information about a seer stone:

"I met with the Twelve at brother Joseph's. He conversed with us in a familiar manner on a variety of subjects, and explained to us the Urim and Thummim which he found with the plates, called in the Book of Mormon the Interpreters. He said that *every man who lived on the earth was entitled to a seer stone, and should have one, but they are kept from them in consequence of their wickedness,* and most of those who do find one make an evil use of it. ***He showed us his seer stone.***" (Brigham Young, *Manuscript History of Brigham Young,* December 27, 1841. Italics and boldface added. Note: This publication does not generally use page numbers, but dates only)

From Martin Harris, we discover that the seer stone was "chocolate-colored" and "somewhat egg-shaped." Further, that the Prophet found this while digging for a well. (B. H. Roberts, *A Comprehensive History of The Church of Jesus Christ of Latter-day Saints,* See Volume 1, pp. 129)

From President Wilford Woodruff, we find out that the Prophet found this seer stone "by revelation some thirty feet under the earth" from the same afore mentioned well (*Wilford Woodruff's Journal,* Volume 8, p. 500; May 18, 1888) [See also B. H. Roberts, *A Comprehensive History of the Church,* Volume 6, p. 230]. Other than the Prophet Joseph having one, we do not have knowledge of any prior prophet having a seer stone.

How Was The
Book Of Mormon Translated?

From the Doctrine and Covenants, we learn that the Prophet Joseph had power given him to translate the Book of Mormon by the means of the *Urim and Thummim.* (See

Section 10:1; 20:8) [See also *History of the Church of Jesus Christ of Latter-day Saints,* by the Prophet Joseph Smith, Volume 1, pp. 19-20]

Oliver Cowdery

The main scribe for writing the Book of Mormon was Oliver Cowdery. He has written these declarative words about the Urim and Thummim:

> "These were days never to be forgotten—to sit under the sound of a voice dictated by the inspiration of heaven, awakened the utmost gratitude of this bosom! Day after day I continued, uninterrupted, to write from his mouth, *as he translated with the Urim and Thummim,* or, as the Nephites would have said, *'Interpreters,'* the history or record called *'The Book of Mormon.'"* (*Messenger and Advocate,* Vol. 1, p. 14; October 1834. Italics added—as printed as a footnote in *Joseph-Smith—History* 1, p. 58)

Elder Orson Pratt

We read these interesting and revealing words of Elder Orson Pratt:

> "The speaker [referring to himself] had been present many times when he [Joseph Smith] was translating the New Testament, and wondered why *he did not use the Urim and Thummim, as in translating the Book of Mormon.* While this thought

passed through the speaker's mind, Joseph, as if he read his thoughts, looked up and explained that the Lord gave him the **Urim and Thummim** when he was **inexperienced in the spirit of inspiration**. But now he had advanced so far that he understood the operations of that Spirit, and **did not need the assistance of that instrument**." (An address, June 28, 1874. Printed in Millennial Star 36:498-499; August 11, 1874. Italics and boldface added)

Seer Stone Used To Translate?

Both Martin Harris and David Whitmer state that sometimes the Prophet Joseph would use the Urim and Thummim as well as the seer stone to translate the Book of Mormon. (See B. H. Roberts, *A Comprehensive History of The Church*, Volume 1, pp. 128-129; See also B. H. Roberts, *Defense of the Faith and the Saints*, 1:257-259, 1907)

Based on this information, the reader will have to decide if more than one instrument was used to translate the Book of Mormon. The prevailing view is that only the Urim and Thummim was the means by which this marvelous work was accomplished. (See Joseph Fielding Smith, *Doctrines of Salvation*, Volume 3, pp. 225-226.)

Where Is The Urim And Thummim?

According to the Prophet Joseph, when he delivered the plates back to the Angel Moroni on May 2, 1838, it is implied that the Urim and Thummim and the breastplate were given back as well. (See *History of the Church,* Volume 1, pp. 18-19. See also Joseph Smith—History 1:60)

President Heber C. Kimball

Regarding the Urim and Thummim, we read an interesting comment from a counselor in the First Presidency, Heber C. Kimball:

"... The question is asked *many times, 'Has brother Brigham got the Urim and Thummim?'* Yes, he has got everything; everything that is necessary for him to receive the will and mind of God to this people. Do I know it? Yes, I know all about it ..." (An address, *Journal of Discourses*, Volume 2, p. 111; August 13, 1853. Italics added)

Did President Brigham Young really have the Urim and Thummim or was it the seer stone? Though a separate instrument, sometimes the seer stone has been referred to as a Urim and Thummim. (See Joseph Fielding Smith, *Doctrines of Salvation*, Volume 3, pp. 222-226; See also, Bruce R. McConkie, *Mormon Doctrine*, 2nd ed., p. 818)

The Manti Temple Dedication

When the Manti, Utah temple was dedicated, it has been stated that the Urim and Thummim was on the altar. From President Wilford Woodruff, we read these revealing words about the private dedicatory services in this holy edifice:

"Before leaving, I consecrated upon the altar the *Seer Stone that Joseph Smith found by revelation some thirty feet under the earth (ground), and carried by him through life.*" (*Wilford Woodruff's Journal*, Volume 8, p. 500; May 18, 1888. Italics added) [See also B. H. Roberts, *A Comprehensive History of the Church*, Volume 6, p. 230; See also, Joseph Fielding Smith, *Doctrines of Salvation*, Volume 3, p. 225]

Elder B. H. Roberts writes that in speaking with President Joseph F. Smith that the Church was in possession of the Prophet Joseph's seer stone. (See *A Comprehensive History of the Church*, Volume 6, p. 231; See also, Joseph Fielding Smith, *Doctrines of Salvation*, Volume 3, p. 225)

In a personal letter written by President Joseph F. Smith, we find out how the Church obtained the Prophet Joseph's seer stone:

Dec. 24th 1882
Dr. Wm. E. McLellan
Independence, Jackson Co. Mo.

The *little stone* you refer to is in *care or possession of Pres. John Taylor.* He having *received it after the death of Pres. B. Young,* who had it in his possession, *he having received it from Oliver Cowdery after he rejoined the Church.* (Joseph F.

Smith of the First Presidency, *Personal Letterbooks*,
p. 438, LDS Church Archives—Ms f 271. Film Reel
#3 Book #2. Italics added)

It is noteworthy that when Oliver Cowdery was
excommunicated from the Church, he took the Prophet's
seer stone; then gave it to President Brigham Young when
he rejoined the Church.

Conclusion

As is written at the beginning of this article, we
know that the Prophet Joseph had a seer stone, but for
what reason, we are not fully informed. We know that the
Church is in possession of it, but beyond this information,
we are left to wonder about its purpose.

* * * * * *

ARTICLE TWENTY

First Vision Accounts

The foundation of The Church of Jesus Christ of Latter-day Saints is the story of the *First Vision*. Of all the mysteries of the gospel, this one has caused countless numbers of people to either decry it or testify of its truthfulness. Accordingly, it is the greatest truth or the greatest fraud. Therefore, let us read a portion of what the Prophet Joseph Smith has declared:

> ". . . I was one day reading the Epistle of James, first chapter and fifth verse, which reads: *If any of you lack wisdom, let him ask of God, that giveth to all men liberally, and upbraideth not; and it shall be given him . . .*
>
> "At length I came to the conclusion that I must either remain in darkness and confusion, or else I must do as James directs . . .
>
> "So, in accordance with this, my determination to ask of God, I retired to the woods to make the attempt. It was on the morning of a beautiful, clear day, early in the spring of eighteen hundred and twenty. It was the first time in my life that I had made such an attempt, for amidst all my anxieties I

had never as yet made the attempt to pray vocally.

"After I had retired to the place where I had previously designed to go, having looked around me, and finding myself alone, I kneeled down and began to offer up the desires of my heart to God. I had scarcely done so, when immediately I was seized upon by some power which entirely overcame me, and had such an astonishing influence over me as to bind my tongue so that I could not speak. Thick darkness gathered around me, and it seemed to me for a time as if I were doomed to sudden destruction."

He then reveals a marvelous manifestation:

"But, exerting all my powers to call upon God to deliver me out of the power of this enemy which had seized upon me . . . just at this moment of great alarm, *I saw a pillar of light exactly over my head, above the brightness of the sun, which descended gradually until it fell upon me.*

"It no sooner appeared than I found myself delivered from the enemy which held me bound. *When the light rested upon me I saw two Personages, whose brightness and glory defy all description, standing above me in the air. One of them spake unto me, calling me by name and said, pointing to the other—This is My Beloved Son. Hear Him!*"

Then, Joseph was given this strict counsel and instruction:

> "... I asked the Personages who stood above me in the light, which of all the sects was right (for at this time it had never entered into my heart that all were wrong)—and which I should join.
> "I was answered that *I must join none of them* ...
> "He again forbade me to join with any of them; *and many other things did he say unto me, which I cannot write at this time* . . ." (Joseph Smith—History 1:11, 13, 14-20. Italics added)

This is the official version of this glorious vision, and it is published for all the inhabitants of the world to read. In addition to this version, there are other accounts that have been printed. Four were researched and published by *BYU* [Brigham Young University] *Studies*, Spring, 1969, on pages 280, 284, 290, and 296. Another version was printed in the *New York Spectator*, September 23, 1843. This version is written in *Dialogue: A Journal of Mormon Thought*, Autumn, 1966, p. 43.

Each of these accounts contain slight variations from the official version, but nothing that has or will cast doubt on the truthfulness of this transcendent event. The reader needs to be reminded that Joseph Smith, Jr. was constantly hated and persecuted for relating this vision. From the official version, we read his moving words:

Reaction To The Vision

"I soon found, however, that *my telling the story* had excited a great deal of prejudice against me among professors of religion, and was the cause of great persecution, which continued to increase; and though I was an obscure boy, only between *fourteen and fifteen years of age,* and my circumstances in life such as to make a boy of no consequence in the world, yet men of high standing would take notice sufficient to excite the public mind against me, and *create a bitter persecution; and this was common among all the sects—all united to persecute me.* (Ibid., verse 22. Italics added)

Based on this knowledge, whenever the Prophet Joseph related the *First Vision,* he was careful how he presented this sacred and holy event and adapted it to the audience he was telling. Accordingly, slight versions arose in order to protect his own person from persecution and bodily harm.

This article will not present these five versions, but will present what early leaders of the Church have spoken on this sacred subject. It is without doubt that these expressions came from the Prophet Joseph himself. They compliment and supplement the official version.

Elder Orson Pratt

From Elder Orson Pratt, we read these insightful words:

"The heavens, as it were, were opened to him

[Joseph], or in other words, a glorious pillar of light like the brightness of the sun appeared in the heavens above him, and approached the spot where he was praying; his eyes were fixed upon it and his heart was lifted up in prayer before the Most High. He saw the light gradually approaching him until it rested upon the tops of the trees. *He beheld that the leaves of the trees were not consumed by it,* although its *brightness,* apparently, was sufficient, as he at first thought, to *consume everything before it.* But the trees were not consumed by it, and it continued to descend until it rested upon him and enveloped him in its glorious rays. *When he was thus encircled about with this pillar of fire* his mind was caught away from every object that surrounded him, and he was filled with the visions of the Almighty, and he saw, in the midst of this *glorious pillar of fire,* two glorious personages, whose countenances shone with an exceeding great lustre.[sic] One of them spoke to him, saying, while pointing to the other, 'This is my beloved Son in whom I am well pleased, hear ye him.'" (*Journal of Discourses,* Volume 12, p. 354; February 24, 1869. Italics added)

"Fire"

Regarding this *"pillar of fire,"* the Lord has revealed:

"And it shall be answered upon their heads;

for the *presence of the Lord shall be as the melting fire that burneth, and as the fire which causeth the waters to boil.*" (D&C 133:41. Italics added)

In addition, the Lord further explains:

"And again, verily, verily, I say unto you, and it hath gone forth in a *firm decree,* by the will of the Father, that mine apostles, the Twelve which were with me in my ministry at Jerusalem, shall stand at my right hand *at the day of my coming in a pillar of fire . . .*" (D&C 29:12. Italics added)

In a later address, Elder Orson Pratt again speaks of the First Vision:

"While thus praying, with all his heart, he [Joseph] discovered in the heavens above him, a very bright and glorious light, which gradually descended towards the earth, and when it reached the tops of the trees which overshadowed him, the brightness was so great that he expected to see the *leaves of the trees consumed by it . . .*"

He then speaks of Joseph's age:

"Mr. Smith had this vision before he was fifteen years old . . ." (*Journal of Discourses,* Volume 17, p. 279; September 20, 1874. Italics added)

Elder John Taylor

We now turn to the expressions of Elder John Taylor:

"He [Joseph] went to the Lord, having read James' statement that 'If any of you lack wisdom let him ask of God that giveth to all men liberally and upbraideth not; and it shall be given him.' He believed that statement and went to the Lord and asked him, and the *Lord* revealed himself to him together with *his Son Jesus*, and, pointing to the latter, said: 'This is my beloved Son, hear him.' He then asked in regard to the various religions with which he was surrounded." (*Journal of Discourses*, Volume 21, p. 161; December 7, 1879. Italics added)

It should not surprise us that God the Father is referred to as the "Lord." Is this not an appropriate name-title of the Father? Is he not the Lord of our Lord?

In a later discourse, Elder Taylor adds this insightful interpretation:

"In the commencement of the work, the Father and the Son appeared to Joseph Smith. And when they appeared to him, the Father, pointing to the Son, said, 'This is my beloved Son, hear him.' As much as to say, 'I have not come to teach and instruct you; but I refer you to my Only Begotten, who is the Mediator of the New Covenant, the Lamb slain from before the foundation of the world; I refer you to Him as your Redeemer, your High Priest and Teacher. Hear Him.'" (*Journal of Discourses,* Volume 26, p. 106; October 20, 1881)

Jesus Christ is our *mediator*. When we say our prayers, we pray to the Father, in the name of the Son. In addition, all of the revelations given in the Doctrine and Covenants are from our Lord; not the Father. Therefore, it is highly appropriate that the Father told the Prophet Joseph, "This is my beloved Son, hear him."

Elder B. H. Roberts

Lastly, we read these interesting expressions from Elder B. H. Roberts:

"In the Spring of 1820, Joseph Smith, in obedience to the instruction given in James—'If any of you lack wisdom, let him ask of God, who giveth to all men liberally and upbraideth not, and it shall be given him'—was praying in the woods to the Father, when he was suddenly enwrapped in a glorious vision. He saw a pillar of light descending from heaven—it rested upon him—its brightness exceeded the brightness of the sun at noon-day. In the midst of this glorious light stood two personages: *each resembling the other.*"

Note these next revealing words:

"*One standing a little above the other*, pointing to the one below him said: *'This is my beloved son; hear ye him.'"* (*Journal of Discourses*, Volume 25, p. 138; January 28, 1884. Italics added)

Does it not seem reasonable to believe that the Father would stand a little above the Son? After all, He is the Father and God of our Lord. (See John 20: 17)

Summation

As was written earlier, these *First Vision accounts* compliment and supplement the official version. There are millions of individuals—including this author—who have prayed to the Father, in the name of the Son, and received a spiritual confirmation that the Father and the Son appeared to Joseph Smith, Jr. in the Sacred Grove and told him not to join any Church. Further, that Joseph Smith is a Prophet, and the first President of The Church of Jesus Christ of Latter-day Saints. Regarding his vision, we conclude by using the words of the Lord's anointed:

". . . I had actually seen a light, and in the midst of that light *I saw two Personages*, and they did in *reality speak to me*; and though I was hated and persecuted for saying that *I had seen a vision*, **yet it was true;**

. . . I knew it, and I knew that God knew it, and I could not deny it, neither dared I do it; at least I knew that by so doing I would offend God, and come under condemnation."(*Joseph Smith— History* 1, verse 25. Italics and boldface added)

* * * * * *

INDEX

as Jesus Christ did, 2; Adam created in the image of, 2; by his valiancy, he was crowned a God, 6; we are children of, 14, was born of woman, 17

Godhead: fullness and power of, 12

Gods: are eternal, 10-12

Gold: 42-45

Gold mine: found in Utah, 44

Gold Plates: 95-96

Grant, Jedediah M: on Christ being a polygamist, 40- 41

Heredity: character comes from spirit rather than, 57

Hill Cumorah: See Cumorah

Hinckley, Gordon B.: A Proclamation To The World, delivered by, 33

Hyde, Orson: on marriage of Christ, 35-36; Christ had wives and children, 35-39

Image of God: Adam created in, 2; man created in, 13

Image of our Eternal parents: all mankind created in, 13

Immortality: Adam and Eve born in, 19

Interpreters: Three Witness promised to see the Urim and Thummim, 92, 93; Nephites called the Urim and Thummim, 98

Jared: See Brother of Jared

Jesus: had power to lay down his body and take it up again, 2-3; laid down his body as his Father did, 3; was naturally begotten, 20-21; conception of not degrading, 24-25; at age twelve, 31-32

Joseph: the husband of Mary, 22-33; had sons and daughters with Mary, 22

Snow, Lorenzo: an inspired couplet, 4-6; couplet idea taught to the Twelve Apostles, 6

Son of God: Adam is a, 13, 15, 18-19; Christ is the, 18-19, 21, 24, 30

Spirit: mortals do not have power to produce a, 15; is elastic, 59-60; no correlation with physical deformities, 60-62

Spiritual Fluid: 63-67; produces spirit children, 66; Christ had both, and blood in his veins, 66-67

Talmage, James E.: spirit and physical deformities, 60, 61

Taylor, John Taylor: a First Vision account, 109-110

Tempter: every earth has its, 8

Testimony: the author's, gained by prayer, 111

Treasures: hidden, 42-46; a seal set upon, 43; can be removed from place to place, 44

Three Witnesses: promised to see the Urim and Thummim, etc., 93

Truth: not always wise to relate all, 31

Universe: age of, 88-90

Urim and Thummim: 91-96; given to the brother of Jared, 93; given to the Prophet Joseph Smith, 93-94; the Three witnesses promised to see the, 93; with the gold plates, 96; called by the Nephites, Interpreters, 98; where is the Urim and Thummim?, 99-100; statement about the, by President Heber C. Kimball, 100

Virgin: Mary was a, 22; Mary ceased being a, 23

Wives: Christ had, 35-41; the Father has a plurality of, 28-29